Early Modern Latin Love Poetry

Latinity and Classical Reception in the Early Modern Period

Editor-in-Chief

Gesine Manuwald (*University College London*)

Associate Editors

Valéry Berlincourt (*University of Geneva*)
Sarah Knight (*University of Leicester*)
Marianne Pade (*Aarhus University*)
Raija Sarasti-Wilenius (*University of Helsinki*)

Volumes published in this Brill Research Perspectives title are listed at *brill.com/rplcs*

Early Modern Latin Love Poetry

By

Paul White

BRILL

LEIDEN | BOSTON

Library of Congress Control Number: 2023932281

Typeface for the Latin, Greek, and Cyrillic scripts: "Brill". See and download: brill.com/brill-typeface.

ISSN 2772-3852
ISBN 978-90-04-54803-9 (paperback)
ISBN 978-90-04-54807-7 (e-book)

This book is printed on acid-free paper and produced in a sustainable manner.

Contents

Early Modern Latin Love Poetry

Paul White
University of Leeds, UK
p.m.white@leeds.ac.uk

Abstract

The majority of early modern authors who wrote Latin verse wrote love poems. They did so in a variety of genres and styles, engaging not only with classical Roman and Greek models, but also with mediaeval and contemporary vernacular traditions of poetry. Their poetry had a transnational dimension, but also needs to be situated within local and national contexts. They used the poetic discourse of love to reflect and comment on wider social, ethical and literary issues, and reconfigured its codes of representation in response to changing conceptions of love in the philosophical and religious spheres. Their poetry often aligned itself with dominant discourses of power and gender, but it could also be subtly subversive or even openly transgressive.

Keywords

love poetry – Neo-Latin – elegy – lyric – epigram – Petrarchism

> Beauty in literature is accidental, depending on the harmony or discord of the words manipulated by the writer, and is not tied to eternity. Epigones, those who frequent already lyricized themes, usually achieve it; innovators, almost never.
>
> JORGE LUIS BORGES, "Literary Pleasure"

Borges – if we may be permitted to wrench his words from their proper context and fit them to our own purpose – might give us reason to doubt the old assumption that the Latin love poetry of the early modern period, being essentially epigonic and imitative in nature, is unworthy of our attention. These poets (so goes an outdated view) languished at the tail end of moribund traditions, or strove to revive long dead traditions they hardly understood, or laboured to translate living traditions into a dead language. In fact, as much recent criticism has shown, the vitality of Neo-Latin love poetry often derives precisely from its creative engagements with traditions both distant and close at hand, and from those poets' clear-eyed understanding of the subtle power of intertextuality to generate new meaning. Even if we disregard the imitative dimension, much of that poetry lives and gives pleasure on its own terms, surprising the modern reader in moments of extraordinary profundity, humour, or perversity – and yes, even beauty.

Most humanists of the Renaissance wrote love poetry of one sort or another. For some, the composition of love poems was central to their literary identity, and was sustained throughout their career; for many, love poetry was just one of the things one would be expected to do at some point, if one wanted to write classicizing verse in Latin. On the one hand, the composition of love poetry was viewed as a fundamentally unserious undertaking, to be contrasted with the weightier, more mature poetry of epic or tragedy – which was both a truism and a conceit to be ironized or subverted. It was done (or was presented as having been done) particularly by poets in their youth, as a matter of both social and literary *decorum*: such poems often appeared in collections entitled "Juvenilia". On the other hand, the composition of love poetry could also be understood as a fundamentally serious endeavour, a mode of writing of universal human significance, capable of reaching towards transcendent spiritual truths.

The universality of the love theme in poetry made its treatments infinitely varied and variable, able to touch both extreme seriousness and extreme unseriousness. Love poetry cannot, of course, be called a literary genre in itself, since erotic themes are present in most – all? – of the classical genres of poetry, spanning lyric, narrative and dramatic modes. Even when we exclude from consideration – as we must, for the purposes of this study – the erotic in narrative, didactic, and dramatic poetry, we are still left with a dizzying array of poetic genres and forms that could be, and were, used for love poetry: elegy, epistle, epigram, ode, hymn, pastoral, satire, and so on. Early modern Neo-Latin poets wrote love poems in all of these genres and forms, and did not necessarily distinguish between them in their publications: love poems (especially epigrams) were likely to feature in miscellaneous collections of *poemata*; equally, collections specifically designated as love poetry were very often polymetric, and they mixed genres.

For an illustration of the metrical and generic variety of what early modern readers recognized as 'love poetry', we can look to compilations such as the *Hortus Amorum* of Aegidius Periander (Frankfurt 1567). The use of the term 'Amores' in the title of this anthology might give the impression that it is a collection of love elegies in the manner of Ovid's *Amores*; actually, the term is not a marker of genre as such, and the Latin title *Amores* had long been used also for collections of love poems in other genres and indeed other languages.[1] The *Hortus Amorum* ("Garden of Loves") anthologized in three volumes Neo-Latin love poems by Italian, German and French authors, with each author section being designated by a flower or plant or animal. The selection of love poems encompassed (among others) epigrams in elegiacs and hendecasyllables, epitaphs and funerary laments, *epithalamia* (wedding songs) in various metres, odes in Sapphics and other Horatian metres, love elegies proper and poems of various other kinds written in elegiacs, *naeniae* ('lullabies'), hexameter pastoral poems, and *epyllia* ('little epics': hexameter poems on mythological erotic themes). Another compilation, the *Veneres Blyenburgicæ, sive Amorum Hortus* of Damasus Blyenburgius (Dordrecht, 1600), covered a similar range of metres and genres. It was arranged like a commonplace book, with excerpts from around 160 Neo-Latin love poets divided into formal and thematic groupings of examples for citation or imitation.

Both because of its generic variety and the sheer scale of its production, Neo-Latin love poetry has perhaps received less unified critical attention than, say, Neo-Latin epic, or tragedy. That is not to say it has been ignored by critics: indeed, studies of individual works of Neo-Latin love poetry are numerous. There have been articles and chapters in collective volumes on the genres in which love poetry was written; on trends within love poetry such as Catullanism and Petrarchism; and on aspects of early modern approaches to love poetry such as obscenity and married love.[2] Surveys of specific poetic genres and modes have appeared in several recent reference works, guidebooks and companions.[3] There have been sections focusing on Neo-Latin love poetry in monographs on the works of specific authors or literary communities, and a handful of book-length studies have been devoted fully to works of Neo-Latin love poetry.[4]

---

1   For example, Boiardo's *Amorum libri tres* (1469–1476) is not, as the title might suggest, a Latin elegiac collection, but an Italian *canzoniere*. Du Bellay's *Amores* (1558) is a Latin collection, but it more closely resembles a book of epigrams (or indeed a sonnet cycle) than it does a classical love elegy book. Later, Petrus Scriverius would give the title *Dominici Baudii Amores* ("The *Amores* of Dominicus Baudius", 1638) to a compilation whose contents were not even limited to poetry: it included letters, orations, disputations, commentaries and poems by authors ancient and modern.

2   On epigram and elegy: Catanzaro & Santucci 1999; de Beer et al. 2009, Cardini & Coppini 2009, Chappuis-Sandoz 2011; on obscenity: Ford & De Smet 1997; on marriage: Galand & Nassichuk 2011, Lionetto 2021; on Petrarchism: Chines et al. 2006, Enenkel & Papy 2006, Coppini & Feo 2012.

3   Parker 2012, Houghton 2013, Enenkel 2014, de Beer 2014, Moul 2015, Cummings 2017, Gaisser 2017, Houghton 2017.

4   Pieper 2008, Ford 2013, Soranzo 2016, de Beer 2013, Wong 2017.

Since Neo-Latin love poems were composed, circulated and published in such a wide variety of ways, often scattered among compositions of quite different kinds, critical attention to them has inevitably been rather patchy and diffuse. It would therefore be impossible to encompass an overview of all Latin love poetry produced in the early modern period. The task becomes somewhat more manageable if limited primarily to the production of Latin love poetry *collections*. From that perspective, we are in a position to identify the main trends and features of such collections, and the genres in which Neo-Latin authors wrote them.

The fact that early modern writers and readers of Latin love poetry did not themselves necessarily make hard-and-fast generic and formal distinctions of the type that might be helpful to modern critics aiming at a systematic overview of the poetic production of the period poses certain challenges for a study of the present kind. It will be necessary to navigate the narrow strait between two threats: first, the risk of over-emphasizing the determining role of 'generic composition' in Neo-Latin love poetry, and second, the danger of defining Neo-Latin poetry solely in terms of *imitatio* of specific classical sources. Both of these tendencies have certainly been a feature of the modern scholarship, some of which has tended either to conceptualize Neo-Latin poetry too restrictively in terms of the classical genres, or to approach it as an exercise in source-hunting. This study does not pretend to avoid completely these pitfalls in the way it is organized: the primary angle of approach to early modern Latin love poetry is via the classical and non-classical sources that informed and shaped it; attention is also given to the diversity of genres and forms that differentiated it; and the discussion is supplemented with some thematic subheadings. This is reflective of two things: the way the criticism has developed, for better or worse, and the basic fact that *imitatio* and genre, though not the be-all and end-all, were undeniably important factors in the way that Latin love poetry defined itself in the early modern period.

It is essential, also, to understand that the models for early modern love poetry in Latin were not only – and sometimes not even primarily – classical. For writers of Neo-Latin love poetry, vernacular traditions loomed just as large as classical Latin traditions, to an extent perhaps greater than for any other Neo-Latin poetic genre. This is largely because of the immense importance of Petrarch and Petrarchism in the period; but the interaction between Latin and vernacular traditions goes beyond this, as we shall see.[5]

---

5   Neo-Latin/vernacular interaction, particularly in the domain of poetry, has been a prominent theme of recent criticism: see e.g. Ford 2013, Deneire 2014, Bloemendal 2015, Winkler & Schaffenrath 2019.

1   Love Elegy

The ancient Roman love elegy was a self-contained genre with clearly defined contours. It had a very restricted canon of authors (Propertius, Tibullus and Ovid), more or less fixed formal characteristics (mid-length poems in elegiacs written from a first-person perspective) and a reasonably coherent thematic focus (the trials and tribulations of the male poet-lover as he strives to win the love of a named woman). It had a set of easily recognizable conventions, images and *topoi*, and a distinctive poetic idiom. All of this would seem to make it an attractive proposition for Neo-Latin imitators who wished to achieve formal and thematic unity in books of love poems.

In fact, the ancient genre was much more ragged at the edges than I have just suggested. The canon of Roman elegists, from an early modern reader's point of view, was not limited to the three named above. Catullus was often grouped together with them, and in the printed editions his poems were frequently conjoined with the elegiac collections of Tibullus and Propertius – probably an artefact of the manuscript tradition.[6] This was not just because Catullus wrote a number of poems in elegiacs, including one (68) which could reasonably be said to be a precursor of the genre of love elegy proper: actually, Neo-Latin writers of love elegy were just as likely to draw on the polymetric Catullus as the elegiac Catullus. There was also the work of Gaius Cornelius Gallus, the first Roman elegist. Although early modern readers knew nothing of his genuine poems, they engaged extensively with those falsely attributed to him: the elegiacs of the sixth-century poet Maximianus (which from 1502 circulated in print under the title *C. Cornelii Galli fragmenta*); and other compositions either forged or innocently misattributed to him.[7] Furthermore, early modern readers saw, quite rightly, that the ancient genre of Roman love elegy was not as bounded or coherent as a narrow reading might suggest, and that Ovid had devoted much of his elegiac writing, beyond the *Amores*, to shifting, blurring and undermining the boundaries of the genre.[8]

Innumerable Neo-Latin love elegies were written, and most Neo-Latin love poets wrote one or more poems recognizably belonging to the genre. These would often appear in miscellaneous publications mixing metres and genres, but there was also a clear trend to compose love elegy *collections*: sequences of elegiac love poems published as artistically arranged books, in which a coherent elegiac persona wrote to and about a pseudonymous *puella* (beloved

---

6   Grant 2019: 19–20.
7   White 2019.
8   The literature on this is vast, but an excellent starting point is Conte 1989.

woman), on the model of the books of Propertius, Tibullus and Ovid. Such collections have attracted some critical interest in the years since Walther Ludwig highlighted the almost complete absence of serious scholarly work on Neo-Latin love elegy.[9]

The 'artistic arrangement' clause in the above definition (which is adapted from Ludwig) opens up some difficult questions. For many Neo-Latin elegy collections, it can be clearly established that artistic arrangement should meaningfully influence our reading of the text, particularly in the case of those published in the print era with authorial paratexts. However, there are also many cases where it becomes much more difficult to speak straightforwardly of 'artistic arrangement', either because the collections as we read them are the product of arrangement by some hand other than the author's, or because the authorial arrangement varied in the course of time: it is exceedingly common to find elegiac collections reissued in different forms, their contents rearranged, augmented or curtailed according to often inscrutable criteria. There are potentially informative comparisons to be made here with ancient poetry books: the classical criticism has long made questions of arrangement a central focus of the study of poetry collections, and they intersect variously with philological, literary, and book history and reception studies perspectives.[10] There has been comparatively less work in this vein on the Neo-Latin poetry book, despite (or perhaps because of?) the fact that there is much more evidence available. Exceptions include work on the way different authorial arrangements of love poetry collections circulating in manuscript give insights into the development of the author's artistic vision and changing attitudes towards certain models or traditions (as well as shifting socio-political allegiances);[11] and work on humanist editors of Neo-Latin love poetry collections in print.[12]

The earliest Neo-Latin love elegy collections were the *Angelinetum* of Giovanni Marrasio (1429), the *Cinthia* of Aeneas Silvius Piccolomini (1423–42), the *Cyris* of Basinio Basini (between 1446 and 1449), and the *Xandra* of

---

9   Ludwig 1976: 172.
10   In the Roman context the most fruitful work on these issues has been in relation to Virgil's
        Eclogues, the *libellus* of Catullus and the *Monobiblos* of Propertius: see van Sickle 1980
        (with other contributions to the same *Arethusa* special issue); Wiseman 1969; Hubbard
        1983; Dettmer 1997. Fantham 2013 provides helpful context. Work on Hellenistic poetry
        collections has provided essential insights (e.g. the essays in Gutzwiller 2005). Almost
        all modern commentary editions of ancient poetry books make at least some effort to
        engage with these questions.
11   E.g. Pieper 2008: 101–117, on Landino's *Xandra*.
12   E.g. Heesakkers 1975 on Petrus Scriverius.

Cristoforo Landino (first circulated *c.*1444). These were love elegy collections in the sense that they maintained a consistent persona across poems mostly addressed to a single named beloved, and in this they were quite clearly and explicitly modelled on the poetry of the classical elegists: they were humanistic love poetry books of a type that cannot be found in mediaeval poetry. This not to say that they excluded mediaeval influence: the *Angelinetum*, for example, draws on troubadour poetry, and all of these early collections (as would many later collections) show a notable Petrarchan influence. Formally, moreover, they differed from the ancient models: on the whole the poems, and the books themselves, were shorter and more epigrammatic than classical elegies.[13]

The *Angelinetum* of Giovanni Marrasio (1400/4–1452) consists of just nine poems, but this slight collection could justly be called the first Neo-Latin love elegy collection.[14] It emerges from the intellectual culture of Siena, where Marrasio knew Aeneas Silvius Piccolomini: indeed, his beloved 'Angela' is portrayed as a member of the Piccolomini family, his poetry as motivated both by love for her and by the urge to sing the praises of that noble family. The collection is also linked to Florence, where Marrasio moved soon after composing the central poems: the sequence is bookended by poems addressed to the great Florentine humanist Leonardo Bruni (*c.*1370–1444). Bruni praised Marrasio as the equal of Propertius, Tibullus and Ovid in love elegy, but what Marrasio offers is a stripped-down version of elegy, depopulated of love gods and Muses, and seemingly hesitating between vernacular traditions of love lyric and the classical themes and tropes he adumbrates. In his dedicatory address to Bruni he writes:

> Quando novi vates ausi sunt tempore prisco
> Carmina, Phoebeos consuluere focos;
> Nunc quaerenda meis non sunt oracla Sibyllae
> Versibus et Phoebus despiciendus erit:
> Tu Cumaea mihi, tu Phoebeaeque sorores,
> Phoebus eris calamis Calliopeque meis.
>
> 1.33–38

---

13   See Donatella Coppini's important remarks on the way these early collections confront the 'closed' formal structure of the epigrammatic book with the 'open' structure of the classical elegiac book (Coppini 2006: 220–227). Also, on the mixing of epigram and elegy in Landino's *Xandra* see Pieper 2009.

14   On the *Angelinetum* see the editions of Resta (Marrasio 1976) and Chatfield (Marrasio 2016); also Landi 2006: 517–524, and Pieper 2008: 78–83 and 2010: 50–56.

> When in ancient times budding poets undertook to compose poetry,
> they consulted the shrines of Apollo; now, my verses do not need to seek
> Sibylline oracles, and they will have no regard for Apollo: you will be my
> Sibyl, you my Muses, you will be Apollo and Calliope for my poetry.[15]

For Marrasio, it is the learned humanist reader and critic – the one whose
genius bridges the ages and brings ancient poetry and learning to a modern
age (1.19–20) – who usurps the role of Muse and inspiration and privileged
reader, a function which in classical elegy is more usually performed by the
puella. Marrasio in his framing poems reconfigures the elegiac discourse to
make it reflect on the relation of his poetry to the literature of the classical
past. From its earliest beginnings Neo-Latin love elegy thus displays a feature
that would be a constant as it developed: a self-consciousness about its own
poetic project.

The poetological dimension of elegy has been a theme of recent criticism
on the Latin love elegies of the *Quattrocento*. The *Eroticon* of Tito Vespesiano
Strozzi (1424–1505), for example, one of the more famous works in the genre,
has attracted approaches that highlight not just the presence of classical allusions and intertexts in his poetry, but the way they are put to work to represent
and define the place of his own poetry in relation to the tradition.[16]

The *Cinthia* of Aeneas Silvius Piccolomini (1405–1464 – the future Pope
Pius II), a collection of 23 poems in elegiacs, exemplifies the mixed character
of early Neo-Latin elegy collections that distinguished them from the classical
elegiac book.[17] The distinction is, though, not entirely clear cut: indeed, the
Cinthia's chief classical model, as the title advertises, is Propertius's *Cynthia*
(his first book of elegies, known as the *Monobiblos*), which it resembles in
number of poems and, to a degree, in their structural arrangement. The mixing
of poems dealing with the love theme with epigrammatic poems on non-erotic
themes is, likewise, also a feature of Propertius 1.

The cycle is framed by poems addressed to Cinthia (1) and to Amor (23),
which give a good sense of how Piccolomini imbues the principal figures of
the elegiac genre – the *puella* and the love god – with metapoetic meaning, and
defines this collection in relation to its classical intertexts.

---

15   Translations mine except where otherwise indicated.
16   See Mindt 2007 on this aspect; also on Strozzi: Murgatroyd 1997, Mesdjian 1997 (the latter
      is also the author of numerous other articles on Strozzi). The work is also a rich source for
      studies of Neo-Latin Petrarchism: Beleggia 2006, and see below pp. 34–35.
17   The *Cinthia* is well studied: see in particular Baca 1972, Galand-Hallyn 1993, Charlet 1997,
      Albanese 1999, Pieper 2008: 83–90, Pittaluga 2011; and for further bibliography Charlet
      2007.

Cinthia, si qua meo debetur fama labori,
  Abs te suscipiam quicquid honoris erit.
Tu mihi das ipsas scribenda in carmina vires,
  Tu facis ingenium, tu facis eloquium.
Te duce concedunt dive in mea vota sorores,
  Te duce Castalio somnia fonte bibo.
Summa tibi, fateor, debentur premia: summo
  Te quoque, si liceat, carmine ad astra feram.
Et nostri prima venies in parte libelli:
  Tu mihi principium, tu mihi finis eris.
    Cinthia 1

Cinthia, if any fame is owed to my work, whatever glory it will have I will get from you.

You give me the very power of writing poetry, you are the maker of my talent, you are the maker of my eloquence. Led by you the divine sisters assent to my prayers, led by you I imbibe dreams from the Castalian spring. The highest rewards are owed to you, I confess: and through the highest poetry, if it is permitted, I will bear you up to the stars. And you will obtain first place in my book: you are my beginning, and you will be my end.

This opening poem is primarily concerned with the role and function of 'Cinthia' in the poetic discourse: it does not dramatize an *innamoramento* scene, nor does it make any attempt to define the features of the beloved or the love relationship itself, nor indeed does it directly express any amorous feeling. The relation between the persona and the *puella* is described in purely poetological terms. Cinthia is defined as the source of the poet's eloquence and the one to whom the poet's *fama* is owed: she is Cinthia and *Cinthia* – the text itself. All of this is a more concentrated and abstracted version of the poem's model, Propertius 1.1 (pointed up by the obvious allusions: line 4 recalls Prop. 1.1.4 "ingenium nobis ipsa puella facit", and line 10 evokes Prop. 1.12.20 "Cynthia prima fuit, Cynthia finis erit."). But Piccolomini has made even more explicit and pervasive than did Propertius the identification of Cinthia with poetry (which, he knows, is implied by her very name, an epithet of the poetry god Apollo): here she leads the Muses and brings the poet to the Castalian spring – a part played in Prop. 3.3 by Apollo himself.

Cinthia is indeed the literal *beginning* of Piccolomini's book (its first word and title, as with Prop. 1), but at its *end* is a poem addressed not to her but to the love god Amor. Interestingly, however, the terms in which the poet entreats

and complains to Amor closely resemble those of the conventional address of
the elegiac lover to his harsh mistress (*dura puella*). It is as if the *puella* and
Amor have exchanged places in the elegiac structure. The switch is completed
in lines 75–82, as the poet claims that it is the *puella*, and not Amor, who has
pierced him – she has taken from him his bow and arrows – and not with
those arrows but with her eyes (cf. Prop. 1.1.1). Piccolomini thus picks up from
Propertius the elegiac discourse's poetological potential but merges and reconfigures elements of it to shape and justify his own recreation of love elegy.

An equally intriguing – though less studied – example of early Neo-Latin
love elegy is the *Cyris* of Basinio Basini (1425–1457).[18] Basinio is (in my view) the
most interesting of the early *Quattrocento* love poets. His poetry is a whirlwind
of motifs from the classical and Petrarchan traditions; the poet-lover persona
runs through them in rapid transitions and elaborates polymorphic fantasies
around them. He is particularly insistent on the idea of the eroticism of reading and writing, whether evoking a reading session together with Cyris where
they press kisses on the poems they are enjoying, or savouring the thought
of Cyris's lips mouthing the words he has written, or even imagining his own
transformation into the love poetry book itself:

> O fierem versus, fierem mea Musa, puella;
>   Quae repetis totiens carmina nostra forem.
> At si non possem versus fore, candida Cyri,
>   Essem purpurea charta recepta manu;
> Meque tui[s] filum rupissent ora labellis,
>   Ora Dioneae digna vigore deae;
> Me ceram premeres placida, mea gloria, palma,
>   Quam modo portasset nostra tabella tibi:
> Omnia perpeterer fieri, modo carpere possem
>   Contactus mollis purpureamque manum.
> Invideo certe nostris, mihi crede, tabellis,
>   Carmina quin etiam nostra beata reor.
> O tibi me lectum mittat fortuna, puella,
>   Infigatque animis pectora nostra tuis.
>   *Cyris* 2.7–20

---

18   One recent study is Pieper 2018; on Basinio's wider œuvre (his elegiac epistolary col-
      lection *Isottaeus* and his epics *Meleagris* and *Hesperis*), see Coppini 2009, Berger
      2002, Schaffenrath 2017. The collection of poems that we call *Cyris* is really a product
      of twentieth-century editing, although it is reasonably likely that they were originally
      intended to form part of a single elegiac book, perhaps with other poems included (see
      Pieper 2018: 123–9).

O would that I could become my verses, become my Muse, darling; would I could be my poems which you repeat so often. And if I could not be my verses, bright Cyris, I would be the page taken up by your beautiful hand; and your mouth would break me, the string, with your lips, a mouth becoming the vigour of Venus; you would press me, the wax, with your gentle palm – my glory – which my tablet had just brought to you: I would endure to become anything, if only I could enjoy your soft touch and beautiful hand. To be sure I envy my tablets, believe me, and even think my poems happy. O may fortune send me to be read by you, girl, and fix my heart in your soul.

Basinio appears to be imagining sending his text to Cyris as a letter in the ancient Roman medium of wax tablets tied together with string (cf. Ovid, *Amores* 1.11 and 1.12 and *Ars Am.* 3.467–498), although the description could just about work to evoke a parchment or paper manuscript sealed with wax and tied with string. Cyris's hand is here twice described as "purpurea", an adjective which might just mean "brilliant" or "beautiful" (it recurs frequently in the collection in this sense), but might also call to mind the image of ink-stained fingers handling a freshly written manuscript. The eroticized descriptions of Cyris's bringing the string to her lips and caressing the words on the wax 'page' with her hand reinforce the association of reading with sexual intimacy. The process of reading and of handling the physical object of the book is here imagined as an ideal merging of selves, more profound even than a sexual union. Basinio develops the idea in the closing lines of the poem, imagining further transformations of the poet-lover: into a tree, into vines, into grapes that might be picked by Cyris and gently trodden by her foot.

The *Xandra* of Cristoforo Landino (1424–1498) is one of the few Neo-Latin love elegy collections to have been the subject of a book-length study, by Christoph Pieper.[19] Both Pieper's book and the monographs by Susanna de Beer and Matteo Soranzo on the poetry of Giannantonio Campano (1429–1477) and Giovanni Pontano (1426–1503) respectively[20] are illustrative of emerging tendencies in Neo-Latin studies in recent years, which track broader trends in literary studies as a whole. Although they continue to be informed by long-established modes of reading Neo-Latin poetry focusing on sources, *imitatio* and intertextuality, they also show a strong awareness of the limitations of those approaches. These studies aim to situate the poetic texts they analyse firmly within social and political contexts, and read them in terms

---

19   Pieper 2008; and see now also McNair 2019 (Ch. 2 on the *Xandra*) and the essays in Kofler & Novokhatko 2016.

20   de Beer 2013 and Soranzo 2016.

of their place and function in the cultural landscape of Florence, Rome and Naples. Their socio-literary approaches are informed by New Historicism and (in Soranzo's case) sociological frameworks deriving from the work of Pierre Bourdieu. Soranzo, indeed, goes so far as to reject 'aesthetic' approaches to poetry entirely in favour of viewing poems as 'acts of cultural identity'. Thus Neo-Latin love poetry (and its composition, dissemination and reception) has come to be seen not just as a rarefied intellectual pursuit but as a stake in strategies of self-fashioning and the acquisition of cultural capital.

The love poetry collections of Landino, Campano and Pontano, in common with the majority of Latin love poetry books written in this period, contain in addition to love poems various other types of poem on non-erotic, social and political themes. Studies whose primary interest is in texts as cultural acts or socio-political interventions might privilege the latter in their analysis at the expense of the former, and risk giving a distorted view of how the collections actually function. On the other hand, the benefit of such studies is that they show that the erotic and the non-erotic poems in these collections are not necessarily distinct groupings of poems with separate motivations, merely thrown together for manuscript dissemination or print publication, but may be thoroughly implicated in one another and together form part of a discourse of self-fashioning. The erotic discourse is folded into the public-facing poetry and vice versa. Propertius in particular furnished a compelling model for Neo-Latin poets who saw the benefit of turning the discourse of erotic elegy towards public themes and the praise of patrons and princes.

To do this required certain contortions and a willingness to accept contradictions and ironies. The Roman elegiac discourse was built on a refusal to engage with grand public themes and the praise of patrons (the rejection of epic and panegyric): this *recusatio* ('refusal') was the gesture – albeit a heavily stylized one – that justified the focus on the erotic and the exclusive devotion of the poetry to the *puella*, both framed as a compulsion rather than a free choice. At the same time, as recent criticism on the ancient Roman elegy has shown, the erotic and the socio-political and public facing dimensions of elegy could be very much bound up with one another. The programmatic *recusatio* theme itself, even while pretending to reject the possibility of political engagement, pointed up political stances which were developed in the poems that followed it. And in the public poetry the elegists made conscious efforts to merge the erotic and the political: in Propertius Book 4, for example, where critics used to see a more or less clear division between the poems with patriotic and aetiological themes and those with erotic themes, now there is greater recognition of the ways they interact with and complicate one another.[21]

---

21   Debrohun 2003.

Far more work has been done on fifteenth-century Italian Neo-Latin love elegy than on the very numerous collections produced beyond the Alps in the sixteenth and seventeenth centuries. Probably the two non-Italian elegists best served by the scholarship are Johannes Secundus (1511–1536) and Petrus Lotichius Secundus (1528–1560), but the former has attracted far more attention for his *Basia* than for his *Elegies*, and the latter's elegies are predominantly non-erotic.[22]

The main features of the love relationship as depicted in the ancient genre were, broadly speaking, present in the versions created by Neo-Latin elegists, though with some modifications and shifts in emphasis. In classical Roman elegy, the poet-lover complains of the hard-heartedness of his beloved, and of the obstacles that stand between them: locked doors, guardians, go-betweens and rivals, and her absences from the city. His poetry is presented, within the discourse, sometimes as a means to overcome these obstacles through persuasion and the poetic imagination, and sometimes as an outlet for his suffering or therapeutic salve. It promises to confer lasting fame on the beloved and, above all, on the poet himself. The beloved, to whom the poet-lover is certainly not married, is characterized as a *puella* (girlfriend) or *domina* (mistress). In the ancient genre her social status is deliberately ambiguous: sometimes she appears to be a married woman whose husband (*vir*) makes efforts to prevent her adulterous dalliances with the elegiac lover; at other times she is more clearly a courtesan figure who demands gifts in exchange for sex, and has many lovers (of whom the *vir* may just be the most favoured one). The scholarship on Roman love elegy since the 1980s has tended to emphasize the metapoetic function of the *puella* in the elegiac discourse, although more recent criticism has turned attention towards social and gender issues.[23]

Most of these features persist in Neo-Latin love elegy, and although some concessions are made to contemporary social realities, the structures of the discourse are essentially similar. In terms of the settings, characters and situations that defined it, the ancient genre had always tended towards stylization or even abstraction: the elegiac world was a place of the artistic imagination in which the poet-lover engaged in dialogue with gods, Muses and his poetic predecessors: this tended to overwhelm the elements of social realism. Equally, though, love elegy was rather unusual among the ancient poetic genres in that its setting was a more or less realistic contemporary urban environment (which

---

22   See in particular the two edited volumes by Auhagen & Schäfer 2001 (on Lotichius; Keith 2001 discusses the erotic elegies) and Schäfer 2004 (which does devote considerable attention to Secundus's *Elegies*); and Murgatroyd's edition of the latter (Secundus 2000). The earlier study of Endres 1981 is somewhat less useful.

23   Wyke 1987 & 1989, Kennedy 1993; James 2003, Miller 2004, Wyke 2007, Greene 2010, Gardner 2013.

provided opportunities for contrasting comparisons with the landscapes, and the underpinning values, of pastoral and epic). Neo-Latin imitators therefore faced a choice whether to set their poems in an elegiac world stripped of markers of cultural specificity, or to write as if the setting of their poems was the Rome of the ancient past, or to update the settings and situations to resonate with contemporary concerns and expectations.

Many Neo-Latin love elegists opted to set their poems in an indeterminate world floating free of the historically and culturally specific anchors that would ground them in their time and place of composition. For long passages they were largely indistinguishable, on this count at least, from classical elegies. There are even rare examples of Neo-Latin elegies whose setting is unambiguously the Augustan Rome of Propertius, Tibullus and Ovid, a world in which gods are worshipped and pagan festivals are observed; they read as a kind of historical fiction (some of the poems of the *Cupidinum libri duo* by Janus Dousa (1545–1604) are of this type). Collections of the third type varied. At one end of the spectrum, we find sequences that reconfigure and transform the entire premises of elegiac love, for example by converting the persona's relationship with the *puella* into a marriage relation underpinned by a Christianized philosophy of love (see below, pp. 74–81). At the other, we find jarring but trivial instances of updating, done (one must assume) for the sake of a joke, such as in the *Elegiae* of Thomas Campion (1567–1620), where Cupid shoots the poet-lover persona not with a bow and arrows but with a gun.[24]

Despite those striking examples of transculturation, on the whole Neo-Latin elegy tended to amplify the tendency towards abstraction and self-reflexivity found in the ancient genre, transmuting social critique into meta-literary comment. Neo-Latin elegists also found it quite natural to merge elements from cognate traditions of love poetry into their elegiac compositions. This worked partly because those traditions had themselves ultimately derived many of their themes and images from classical elegy, and so it did not seem inappropriate to reabsorb them into the discourse. It also worked because the elegiac discourse, despite its apparent formulaic restrictiveness, had always been very ready to appropriate elements from other genres and traditions to itself, or to engage in dialogue with them, or to mark them out for scrutiny. In other words, love elegy was a genre defined by its intertextuality, which made it an attractive proposition for Neo-Latin poets.

One of the defining themes of the classical genre was *servitium amoris* (the 'slavery of love'), which found expression, broadly speaking, in two ways. First was the conceit – traditional in ancient poetry and by no means an innovation

---

24   Moul 2013: 309–10.

of the Roman genre – that the poet-lover was a slave to the all-powerful, cruel and capricious love god himself, an idea crystallized in the image of the lover as a captive in chains in a triumphal procession led by Amor.[25] Second, and more specific to Roman love elegy, was the idea of the poet-lover being enslaved to his mistress – the term *domina* itself evokes the sense of *slave*-mistress – and living in a state of powerless degradation and (sometimes sexualized) humiliation because of this. This latter expression of the idea – or at least the elevation of the conceit into a theme or *topos* – seems to have been an innovation of the Augustan elegists, with few precedents in ancient poetry.[26]

It has often been observed that the elegiac *servitium amoris* shares affinities with the conventions of troubadour *fin amor* and of Petrarchan love, according to which the lover adopts a pose of self-abasement and supplication before his exalted, idealized beloved.[27] It would of course be reductive to view the elegiac *servitium* as the sole literary origin and model for this characterization of the beloved and of the love relationship in the *fin amor* tradition, or to view the latter as a straightforward adaptation of the ancient *topos* to new social and religious contexts.[28] The social hierarchies on which the conceit depends have fundamentally different associations and emotional valences: to use the language of feudal vassalage to describe a love relationship has very different implications from evoking the Roman institution of slavery (and the real threat of captivity in military defeat). Moreover the religious dimension that developed in the *dolce stil nuovo* and Petrarchan love poetry gives the elevation of the beloved a metaphysical significance that is simply not there in classical elegy.

Another key difference is that the elegiac *domina* is often depicted as taking a cruel pleasure in tormenting the poet-lover; her dominance has an element of flirtation, and sex is not out of the question. This is far from the idealized, distant Petrarchan beloved, who does not reciprocate the poet-lover's desire, except in ambiguous ways. In Petrarchan poetry, the lover's abasement is expressed as a profound mental distress, whereas in elegy it is more likely to be playfully masochistic and eroticized.

These distinctions, however, did not prevent Neo-Latin elegists from merging models in their treatments of the *servitium amoris* topos. This from Piccolomini's poem on the theme:

---

25   Ovid, *Amores* 1.2.23–52; and see below, p. 35, for Neo-Latin imitations of this scene.
26   Lyne 1979; but see also Murgatroyd 1981 for other precedents in Greek and Roman poetry.
27   E.g. Pieper 2010: 46–7.
28   See Whittington 2016: 82–113 for a nuanced account.

Ast ego quid sit amor, quid dura incendia novi
    Et quot mortifero sint in amore doli;
Et tamen infelix iterum compellor eodem,
    Cogor et antiquo subdere colla iugo.
Tantum sola potes in me, que sidere quo vis,
    Cinthia, me ducis, Cinthia, meque trahis.
Stare tua haud contra possum vel tela vel artes
    Et si me ludis, ludier usque iuvat.

      Cinthia 16.5–12

But I know now what love is, and its harsh fires, and how many decep-
tions there are in death-bringing love; and yet I am driven again in my
misery to the same point, and I am forced to submit my neck to the yoke
of old. You alone have power over me, you, Cinthia, who lead me and pull
me, Cinthia, by whatever star you will. I can hardly stand firm against
either your weapons or your wiles, and if you toy with me, I even take
pleasure in being toyed with.

The poem is mainly an expression of *servitium amoris* in the Propertian manner (and is clearly a reformulation of Prop. 3.11.1–4).[29] It is typical of the way the
classical genre characterizes the *domina* and the suffering she imposes on the
lover, including the idea that her mastery over him and the torment she causes
are a source of pleasure for him (and perhaps for her too). At the same time
Piccolomini evokes a Petrarchan model, the sonnet "S'amor non è, che dunque
è quel ch'io sento?", an exceedingly popular point of reference for Neo-Latin
love poets (on which see below, pp. 36–38).[30] Thus Piccolomini aligns the elegiac *servitium* to the *domina* with the specifically Petrarchan motif of pleasurable suffering (*voluptas dolendi*).

    In ancient Roman love elegy, the theme of love's soldiery (*militia amoris*)
was, in part, an extension of the anti-militarism of the *recusatio*: it developed
the claim to superiority of love over war and of love elegy over martial epic.
Its emblematic treatment was Ovid *Amores* 1.9 ("All lovers are soldiers, and
Cupid has his own camp"); but that poem is essentially parodic, in that it rhetorically extends and particularizes aspects of an established theme to make
an amusingly paradoxical argument. In the work of the earlier Roman elegists,
the theme is mainly used to draw a moral contrast between military service
and service in love's army (which is not always unequivocal), and is related

---

29   Albanese 1999: 140–1.
30   On the parallels to Petrarch *Canz.* 132, see Landi 2006: 525–6.

more directly to their own experiences: Tibullus probably served in Gaul with Messala (1.7.9–12), and his predecessor Gallus, represented in Virgil's *Eclogues* as a soldier-poet, was in the forged Aldine elegy[31] depicted as a love poet on active duty in the Parthian campaign of Publius Ventidius.

In Neo-Latin love elegy, the anti-militaristic arguments associated with *militia amoris* are often damped down in favour of more schematic treatments of the theme in the lineage of *Amores* 1.9. Where there is an element of anti-establishment critique, it is more likely to be an expression of anti-aulic themes and the conventional opposition of public and private or city and country, rather than anti-militaristic themes per se. The anti-militaristic component of the *recusatio* is often minimized or neutralized entirely when confronted with the exigencies of dedication to patrons and rulers. Thus it is common to see Neo-Latin love elegists doing at length precisely what they claim to be unable or unwilling to do: Remacle d'Ardennes (Remaclus Arduenna, *c.*1480–1524), for example, in his first elegy (*Amorum libri tres* 1.1 (1513)) asserts that when he first met his beloved Iordana, sorrowful Elegy forbade him to engage in warfare and the writing of militaristic poetry, but then intersperses his treatment of the *militia amoris* theme with praise of the military exploits of Maximilian and Charles, and concludes the poem with a promise to fight, and sing of, war in the future. By 1520 the Emperor had granted him the title of court historiographer.[32] The demands of political careers meant that many humanist love poets could not in their poems fully commit to the conceit of erotic *otium*. Filippo Buonaccorsi (known as 'Callimachus', 1437–1496) a smooth operator in the Polish court of Casimir IV, included in his *Elegiarum libellus ad Fanniam Sventhocam* a *recusatio* poem (17) in which he does at extraordinary length what he claims to be unable to do: namely to sing the praises of the Polish king as military leader.[33]

The conceit of *militia amoris* was thus often used as a pretext for praise of the military exploits of the patron or ruler to whom the poetic book was dedicated ('though I am only fit to be a soldier in love's army, you ...'); or as a way of giving the praise but in the future tense or subjunctive mood ('If it were permitted to me, I would sing your exploits x, y, and z ...').

Other Neo-Latin poets found ingenious ways of reformulating the elegiac rejection of high politics and of the waging of wars as a less provocative proposition. Cristoforo Landino's *Xandra* 3.1, a poem of dedication to Piero de' Medici, gives what appears to be a conventional elegiac list of military themes

---

31 ps.-Gallus 1588. On which see White 2019: 38–58.
32 Bietenholz & Deutscher 2003: 140.
33 On Callimachus in the Polish court, see Segel 1989.

he refuses to treat in his poems (3.1.9–14), but his point is that it is really peace-time statesmanship that deserves praise – the *castra* yields to the *toga* – thus consolidating the image of Piero as prudent citizen statesman that Landino wished to promote.[34]

Another Florentine love elegist (and follower of Landino), Ugolino Verino (1438–1510), began the second book of his love elegy collection *Flametta* with a conventional *excusatio* for preferring love to war (addressed to Lorenzo de' Medici), but ended it with a poem reasserting the pre-eminence of the war theme over that of love. The farewell to love and to elegy (*finis amandi*) was a feature of the closing poems of the ancient love elegy books (cf. Prop. 3.25, Ovid *Am.* 3.15). Many Neo-Latin elegists used it to reverse the premises of the elegiac rejection of war and public life. This is partly an expression of the conventional idea that love poetry was reserved for youth, and must be abandoned at the point of maturity for more serious themes; it is also a way for Neo-Latin poets to please their patrons and promote their own careers. Verino's treatment of the 'farewell to elegy' is an explicit abandonment of the entire metaphorical apparatus of *militia amoris*:

> Aurea, cede, Venus, tuque, o formose Cupido,
>   Vestraque de campo vellite signa meo.
> Area maior equis iam nunc pulsetur anhelis,
>   Non sunt imbelli grandia danda lirae.
>   *Flametta* 2.55

Golden Venus, give way, and you too, handsome Cupid, and remove your standards from my field. Now let a larger ground be pounded by the panting horses; great subjects should not be given to an unwarlike lyre.

In commanding Venus and Cupid to retreat from the field, Verino banishes elegy's politically disruptive metaphors to restore a kind of 'order' to his poetic vision – that of epic.

Some Neo-Latin love elegists did address in their poems real experiences of warfare: Basinio (*Cyris* 8) casts himself as an elegist in the midst of arms, caught up in the siege of the castello di Guardasone in 1449. Lotichius frequently adopts in his elegies the persona of a soldier on active service, and he did indeed fight in the Schmalkaldic War (1546–7). But more often the theme of soldiery and warfare serves as a basis for metaphorical elaborations

---

34   Further on the ways Landino positions his elegiac book in relation to Piero and to Florentine cultural and political power: Coppini 2006: 214–220; Pieper 2008: 193–309.

of the love theme, on the model of Ovid *Amores* 1.9. Janus Dousa's *Cupidines* 1.3 offers a twist on the conceit that the male poet-lover is the soldier in love's army: instead it is the *puella* who is imagined as the rampaging soldier, and the poet-lover is the body being pillaged. Dousa extends the conventional metaphors, images and themes of love elegy as far as they will go, elaborating them in extreme and graphic detail. The violence implicit in the elegiac themes of *servitium amoris* and *militia amoris* is brought to an extreme pitch, as the metaphors of the soldiery and servitude of love explode into images of pillage, execution, murder: love's suffering is physical violence on bodies; love is not a sweet death but a kind of bloody slaughter, a carnage. We know that love burns, but Dousa's persona rips out his scorched heart and presents it to Cupid as a burnt offering from which he may re-light his torch in order to ignite the unyielding *domina* (1.1). These are baroque extravagances worthy of d'Aubigné, but they are rooted in Latin love elegy itself, or in how the later sixteenth-century elegists viewed the genre.

A defining theme of elegy was the *exclusus amator* (shut-out lover), given expression in the form of the poetic set-piece known as the *paraklausithyron* (song outside of the locked door).[35] The locked door is the emblematic physical manifestation of the many social and psychological barriers that stand between the elegiac lover and erotic fulfilment: it concretizes the dynamic that motivates and structures the elegiac discourse. The poet-lover's song, addressed to the door itself, or to a guardian (*ianitor*), or to the *puella* behind the door, is both a lament and an attempt to persuade: the two key (intradiscursive) functions of elegiac love poetry. The theme is frequently taken up in Neo-Latin elegy, sometimes with interesting adjustments to accommodate it to contemporary social situations. In the *Amores* of Joachim Du Bellay (*c.*1522–1560), for example, the *puella* Faustina is depicted in the second poem (*Raptus Faustinae*) as having been stolen away from him and locked up by her husband; the poet-lover persona addresses a lament to the door of the house in which her husband has confined her (*Ad ianuam Faustinae*). This is the conventional elegiac situation. However, in other poems in the collection Du Bellay modifies the situation so that instead Faustina has now been forced to "enter the cloisters of a holy house", i.e. a convent ("sacrae ... claustra subire domus"). The term "claustra" (bolt or locked door, but also "cloisters") recurs in subsequent poems in the collection; it is a word that evokes the classical elegiac situation but also designates a social institution of the contemporary Rome that is the setting for Du Bellay's collection. The merging of the ancient elegiac discourse into the modern setting is highlighted in the poem entitled

---

35   Propertius 1.16, Tibullus 1.2 and 1.5, Ovid *Amores* 1.6, 2.2 and 2.3.

Cum Faustina inclusam esse Venerem et Amorem ("That Venus and Cupid were imprisoned together with Faustina"):

> Claustra tenent nostram (sic Dii voluere) puellam:
>> Foelix quem clausum ferrea claustra tenent.
> Illic sunt Charites lususque iocique leporesque,
>> Et quicquid sedes incolit Idalias.
> Casta Venus sancto corpus iam velet amictu,
>> Sacraque iam discat relligiosus Amor.

Bolts [*or*: cloisters] confine my girl (so the gods willed it): happy the one imprisoned by those iron bolts. There the Graces are, and frolics, and laughter, and delights, and whatever dwells in the Idalian abode. Venus should now be chaste and veil her body with a holy habit, and Cupid should now be a monk studying theology.

In imagining the pagan love gods entering the convent and adopting the garb of nun and monk, Du Bellay is not celebrating the triumphant Christianization of pagan erotic poetry; rather, pagan eroticism infiltrates the sacred place in the guise of religiosity. The convent becomes a space of sexual fantasy, and the language used to evoke this fantasy – *lususque iocique leporesque* – is the language of a specific poetic aesthetic: Neo-Catullanism.

2   Neo-Catullanism

Catullus became a near ubiquitous presence in Neo-Latin love poetry, imitated perhaps more than any other single poet of antiquity, with the exception of Ovid. The imitation of Catullus was immensely varied, reflecting both the remarkable influence of his short collection and the sheer variety of erotic themes, stances and styles that it contained. The poems of the Catullan *libellus* are of course by no means exclusively erotic in theme, but the repeated and widespread imitation of those few that are made his influence into a phenomenon: not Catullus, but Catullanism. Catullus wrote love poetry in hendecasyllables, in Sapphics and in elegiacs; he wrote poems celebrating the joys of love and tender poems of loss; he wrote of illicit sex and of the bonds of marriage; he wrote violent and obscene invective and light and jokey poems of friendship. He offered models for imitation to the epigrammatist, the elegist, the author of lyrics, and the composer of *epithalamia*.

The most authoritative general guide to the Renaissance reception of Catullus remains Gaisser 1993; and numerous studies since have enriched our understanding of specific instances and developments of Catullan reception in love poetry.[36] The poems of Catullus had been rediscovered around 1300; in the fifteenth century he became established as a model for Neo-Latin poets, and by the sixteenth century Catullanism was a discourse central to the composition of Latin love poetry.

Giovanni Gioviano Pontano (1429–1503) was one of the first to imitate Catullus's love poetry at length, in the collections *Pruritus* (1449), *Parthenopaeus* (1457) and *Baiae* (ca.1500), and thus to establish neo-Catullanism as a style.[37] His early poems, like those of his fellow Neapolitan court poet Antonio Beccadelli (known as Panormita (1394–1471); on whom see below pp. 82–84) were largely written in imitation of Martial; but whereas Beccadelli's engagements with Catullus remained indirect and superficial, Pontano clearly read him extensively, and his imitations of Catullus have great depth and complexity. The features of the style are most evident in poems written in that most characteristic Catullan metre, the hendecasyllable.

Ad pueros de columba
Cui vestrum niveam meam columbam
Donabo, o pueri? Tibine, Iuli,
Num, Coeli, tibi, num tibi, Nearche?
Non vobis dabimus, mali cinaedi;
Non vos munere tam elegante digni.   5
Quin ite, illepidi atque inelegantes;
Ales nam Veneris nitore gaudet,
Odit sorditiem inficetiasque,
Insulsos fugit et parum venustos.
Sed cuinam cupis, o columba, munus   10
Deferri? Scio; nam meam puellam
Amas plus oculis tuis, nec ulla
Vivit mundior elegantiorve.
Haec te in delitiis habebit, haec te
Praeponet nitidis suis ocellis,   15

---

36   Gaisser 1993 builds on the foundation of Ludwig 1989a and 1990 for the early development of the style in Neo-Latin poetry; consult also Morrison 1955, Baier 2003, Ford 2013: 55–96, Wong 2021.

37   Baier 2003 and Gaisser 2015.

Nec tanti faciet suam sororem.
Huius tu in gremio beata ludes,
Et circumsiliens manus sinumque
Interdum aureolas petes papillas.
Verum tunc caveas, proterva ne sis;   20
Nam poenas dabis et quidem severas,
Tantillum modo tam venusta poma
De tactu vities: et est Diones
Tutelae hortulus ille dedicatus;
Numen laedere tu tuum caveto.   25
Impune hoc facies, volente diva,
Vt, cum te roseo ore suaviatur
Rostrum purpureis premens labellis,
Mellitam rapias iocosa linguam,
Et tot basia totque basiabis,   30
Donec nectarei fluant liquores.
  Parthenopaeus 1.5

To some boys, about a dove
To which of you shall I give my snow white dove, boys? You, Julius, or
you, Coelius, or you, Nearchus? We shall not give it to any of you wicked
catamites; you are not worthy of such an elegant gift. Go then, charmless
and inelegant boys; for the bird of Venus rejoices in brightness, hates filth
and rudeness, and shuns those who are coarse and without charm. But
you, dove, to whom do you want to be given as a gift? I know: for you love
my girl more than your own eyes, and there is none alive more neat and
elegant than her. She will make you her favourite, she will prefer you to
her own bright eyes, and will not value her own sister as much as you. You
will play happily in her lap and, leaping about, will thrust at her hands
and bosom and sometimes her pretty golden breasts. But do be careful
then not to be too forward; for you'll pay the penalty and it'll be a serious
one, should you injure, by your touch, such charming fruits even in the
slightest: and that little garden down there is vowed to the protection of
Venus: beware of harming your own deity. You will do this unpunished,
if the goddess wills it, so when she kisses you with her rosy mouth press-
ing your beak to her beautiful lips, you may playfully snatch her honeyed
tongue, and you'll kiss so, so many kisses, till the streams of nectar flow.

This poem has almost all the hallmarks of the Catullan style, from the frequent use of diminutives (*papillas, hortulus, labellis*) and the accumulations

of comparative expressions (*mundior elegantiorve*), to the vocabulary marking specifically Catullan aesthetic concepts and their negations (*venusta, iocosa* versus *illepidi, parum venustos, insulsos*). The repetition with variation of the expression at line 12 then 15 is Catullan – such repetitions are characteristic of the hendecasyllabic style – as is the expression itself (Cat. 3.5). There are numerous allusions to specific poems of Catullus: the opening lines evoke the dedication of the *libellus* (Cat. 1.1) and the invective of Cat. 16.2, but the poem's main theme is clearly taken from the poems on Lesbia's pet sparrow (Cat. 2 and 3), and its conclusion imitates the kiss poems (Cat. 5, 7 and 99). Distinctively Catullan words mark the borrowings: *circumsiliens* (Cat. 3.9); the verbs for kissing *suavior* and *basio*; and, emphatically, the line *et tot basia totque basiabis* (= Cat. 7.9 "tam te basia multa basiare").

It is likely that few readers will have missed the point that Pontano's *columba* is not really a dove (or that the fluid at the poem's climax is not really nectar). Much less obvious is the idea that the sparrow in the poem's model, Cat. 2 and 3, was also meant to be a penis (a reading that is by no means universally accepted today); but as Gaisser has shown, Pontano was reading those poems through the lens of Martial 11.6, and did not need to wait for Angelo Poliziano (1454–1494) to make the reasoned case for the obscene reading. In any case, in Pontano's version the *double entendre* is quite obvious from the outset, even to readers to whom such a reading of Catullus's sparrow had never occurred, or who had never so much as read Catullus 2 or 3 or Martial 11.6.[38]

The purely stylistic features of neo-Catullanism outlined here were by no means restricted to direct imitations of Catullus in hendecasyllables: they can be found, in varying doses, and in less ostentatious applications, in most kinds of Neo-Latin love poetry. Wong's argument that the poets who employed the neo-Catullan style were doing something self-consciously "alternative" or non-mainstream[39] is plausible in some individual cases, and is perhaps truer early in the period, when Catullanism was being rejected by authors like Mantuan for moral and aesthetic reasons, than it is later; but features of the Catullan style eventually became so standard in Neo-Latin love poetry that they were simply part of the fabric of the language of love in Latin, and signified nothing in particular about a poet's attitudes or allegiances.

Pontano is the most thoroughly Catullan of the love poets of the *Quattrocento*. His younger contemporary and friend in Naples, Michael Marullus (1453–1500), is often mentioned in the same breath as Pontano in this context, though his poetic *œuvre* in Latin is less insistent on the Catullan model. Among Marullus's

---

38   Discussions of this poem: Gaisser 2012: 181–2; Wong 2021: 327–8.
39   Wong 2021: 319.

epigrams (first published in two books in 1488–9, then as four books in 1497)
are several addressed to a 'Neaera', in which Catullan language and themes are
sometimes combined with spiritual and philosophical ideas, which would be a
more central concern of his famous *Hymni naturales* (1497).[40] Marullus's love
poetry represents what Philip Ford called "the soft version of neo-Catullan
poetry" (to be distinguished from the "hard" version of Beccadelli and the
"medium" kind typified by Sannazaro).[41] It is softer both in the sense that
it minimizes the sexual elements and in that it largely eschews the stylistic
showiness – though not always, as the following example demonstrates:

> Salve, nequitiae meae, Neaera,
> Mi passercule, mi albe turturille,
> Meum mel, mea suavitas, meum cor,
> Meum suaviolum, mei lepores,
> Te ne vivere ego queam relicta?
> Te ne ego sine regna, te sine aurum
> Aut messes Arabum velim beatas?
> O prius peream ipse, regna et aurum!
>
>   *Epig.* 1.2, "Ad Neaeram"

Greetings Neaera, my wicked temptress, my little sparrow, my little white
turtledove, my honey, my sweetness, my darling, my kisses, my delight.
If I were to leave you, could I go on living? Without you could I desire
kingdoms, gold or the rich harvests of the Arabs? Oh! May I perish first,
kingdoms and gold along with me.[42]

This slight epigram won a perhaps surprising degree of fame and influence,
imitated by Secundus, Ronsard, and many others; Julius Caesar Scaliger
(1484–1558), who could not quite see its success as deserved, devoted a lengthy
discussion to it in his *Poetices libri septem* (book 6, ch. 4), and suggested
improvements.

A cursory reading of the *Basia* ("Kisses") of Johannes Secundus (1511–1536)
might leave one with the impression that it is merely a collection of ingenious

---

40   Rees 2018.

41   Ford 2013: 60.

42   Marullus 2012: 2–3. Translation by Charles Fantazzi. See also the discussion of this epi-
      gram by Auhagen 2008, arguing that Marullus is here announcing his preference for a
      chaster version of Catullus by reclaiming the term 'sparrow' in its non-obscene meaning.

exercises de style, an attempt to exhaust the possibilities for imitation of a handful of short poems of Catullus by running them through all the metrical and stylistic variations.[43] But this slender book – just 19 short poems – is far richer and far more innovative than that that description would suggest. It was a true literary phenomenon of the sixteenth century, sparking as it did an explosion of imitations in the same vein, and popularizing the neo-Catullan style throughout Europe. It remains today the most often edited and the most frequently discussed Neo-Latin love poetry collection.[44]

As we have seen, Neo-Latin poets had written Catullan 'kiss' poems before Secundus: several appear in Pontano's *Parthenopaeus* and other collections. Such poems were also being written in vernacular languages before the publication of Secundus's *Basia*.[45] But Secundus was the first to compose a cycle of poems on the theme, which gave him scope to develop the link between kissing and poetry, and to play on the equivocation between erotics and poetics.

> Non sunt certa meam moveant quae basia mentem,
>   uda labris udis conseris, uda iuvant;
> nec sua basiolis non est quoque gratia siccis,
>   fluxit ab his tepidus saepe sub ossa vapor.
> [...]
> Qualia sed sumes, nunquam mihi talia redde:
>   diversis varium ludat uterque modis.
> At quem deficiet varianda figura priorem,
>   legem submissis audiat hanc oculis,
> ut, quot utrimque prius data sint, tot basia solus
>   dulcia victori det, totidemque modis.
>
>   *Basia* 10.1–4, 17–22

The kisses that excite me are not of fixed type: press wet kisses on wet lips, and I like wet kisses. Nor are dry kisses without their own charm too:

---

43   The primary models for the theme are Catullus 5 and 7, together with the Juventius 'kiss' poems 48 and 99; but many other Catullan poems also furnish source material.

44   See in particular Schoolfield 1980, Godman 1988, Price 1996, Balsamo & Galand-Hallyn 2000, Guillot 2011, Wong 2017. The text of the *Basia*, being short, can be found in numerous 'editions' and translations. Guillot's edition and commentary (Secundus 2005) is not entirely satisfactory; we await eagerly the new edition of Secundus's complete works which is currently in preparation under the direction of Perrine Galand and Virginie Leroux.

45   On Secundus's Italian Neo-Latin models see Galand 2010; on the French context see Ford 1993 and 2013.

from these a languid warmth has often streamed deep into my bones. [...]
But whatever kind you receive, never give me back the same kind: let's
both play a game of variation with different styles. The first one who fails
to vary the form should obey, with downcast eyes, the following law: that
however many kisses were already given, the loser alone should give just
as many sweet kisses to the winner, and in just as many styles.

Secundus extends the Catullan conceit of the lovers' game of counting kisses,
making of it a game of erotic variation. In doing so, he brings out more explicitly the metapoetic dimension of the kissing game, playing, as he often does in
the collection, on the identification of the *basium* as kiss with the *Basium* as
poem. The terms used to describe the different styles (*modi*) of kissing and the
idea that their form must be varied (*varianda forma*) are drawn from the met-
alanguage of poetry, and the formulation in the opening line *mentem movere*
neatly encapsulates both the erotic and the poetic meanings: the varied *basia*
both "excite the senses" and "stimulate the intellect". The poem, then, works as
a general statement of the desirability of *variatio* as a key aesthetic principle in
poetry (as it had been for the Hellenistic and Roman poetry books that humanist poets took as their models). It also highlights the way that principle works
in the very book of *Basia* to which the poem belongs. The poems that make
up the collection are indeed written in a variety of different metres (another
meaning of "diversis ... modis" in line 18): eight distinct metrical forms in total,
adding to the metres of the Catullan poems on which the text is modelled
(hendecasyllable and elegiac couplet) a range of Horatian lyric metres (alcaics,
the lesser asclepiad, anacreontics, glyconics with pherecrateans, and iambic
variations). In the hands of Secundus the love poetry book thus becomes a
display of virtuosity and a showcase for creative imitation, embracing *contaminatio* (combined imitation from a variety of different sources and genres).

The influence of Secundus's *Basia* on vernacular and Neo-Latin poetry in
northern Europe was both immediate and long-lasting. In the first instance it
was taken up as a model by French poets, in the intellectual circles of Lyon and
then among the Pléiade poets, writing primarily in French but also – in the
case of Du Bellay – in Latin. Its status as a modern classic was consolidated in
the latter part of the sixteenth century by Latin poets from the Low Countries
and France who wrote complete books of *Basia* in imitation of Secundus:
Janus Lernutius (1545–1619), Janus Dousa (1545–1609) and Jean Bonnefons
(1554–1614). These collections together with that of Secundus served as models
for numerous vernacular imitators throughout northern Europe in the seventeenth century.

3   *Excursus*: Art and Life

It is convenient at this point to address the issue of biographical approaches to love poetry in the scholarship. Viewed from our perspective, it may seem odd that such single-minded attention has been given by critics over the centuries to pinning down the poetry to elements of the poet's biography, and to the central question of the 'real identity' of the women to whom poets addressed their compositions. This was until relatively recently a persistent preoccupation of scholarship on Catullus and the Roman elegists. And Neo-Latin scholarship followed suit, expending disproportionate energies on speculation about the identity of the real women behind the pseudonymous *puellae*. The efforts do seem all the more disproportionate in the case of the many Neo-Latin compositions that are ostentatiously imitative and fictive. When reading much of the older scholarship, it is often difficult to see what benefit there could be in seeking distinct identifications for the many Neaeras, Candidas and Cynthias that populated the pages of Neo-Latin poetic books, especially where such investigations are not set within broader frameworks of interpretation.[46] Equally, though, reducing the love relationships depicted in Neo-Latin poetry to the status of pure fiction, and the Neo-Latin elegiac *puella* to a mere cipher or paper creation, risks closing off potentially fruitful avenues of enquiry. Recent research has enabled more sophisticated approaches: clearly it is a category error to read Neo-Latin love poems as straightforward documents of lived experiences, but it may also be a mistake to see them exclusively as products of bookish invention and *imitatio* with no extratextual referents.[47]

Indeed, many Neo-Latin love poets more or less explicitly identified the pseudonymous *puellae* whom they addressed in their poetry with real women. This fact need not lead us down the blind alley of naive biographicism. The purposes for which they did so varied. Often it was to do with the socio-literary functions of the work (as with Marrasio's 'Angela'); sometimes it had a thematic significance: for example, that Jean Salmon Macrin's 'Gelonis' is Guillone Boursault, his wife, has a bearing on the distinctive style and character of his *Epithalamiorum liber*. The case of Giannantonio Campano's book of love elegies to Diana is particularly notable, since the 'Diana' it addressed certainly

46 For example, on the unfortunate preoccupation with the identity of the 'Neaera' of Marullus's love poetry, see Lamers 2009: 191–2 criticizing Kidwell 1989.
47 There has been a parallel development within Classics, with some critics reacting against the more extreme applications of *persona* theory to restore biographical reading to the interpretation of ancient poetry: the category of 'autofiction' is useful here. See e.g. Goldschmidt 2019.

was a real woman (Margherita da Montesperello), but the love relationship it depicted was openly fictional.[48] Campano had been commissioned to write the poems by the Perugian condottiere Braccio Baglioni. Instead of writing love poems *in persona* of Braccio or in the third person, Campano mostly writes in the first person of his own love for Diana (which he freely admits to be simulated), sometimes figuring the relation between himself and Braccio as one of elegiac rivalry, at other times as that of patron to poet. The result is a lover's discourse that shifts easily back and forth between the fictive situation of elegiac love and the social reality that underpins it.

A famous passage in Apuleius has, over the centuries, provided a justification for biographical approaches to Latin love elegy; and it shows that ancient readers, too, had been preoccupied by the question of the true identity of the elegiac *puellae*, even if Ovid had been at pains to deflect them.

> Hic illud etiam reprehendi animadvertisti, quod, cum aliis nominibus pueri vocentur, ego eos Charinum et Critian appellitarim. Eadem igitur opera accusent C. Catullum, quod Lesbiam pro Clodia nominarit, et Ticidam similiter, quod quae Metella erat Perillam scripserit, et Propertium, qui Cynthiam dicat, Hostiam dissimulet, et Tibullum, quod ei sit Plania in animo, Delia in versu.
>
> *Apologia* 10

> On this point, you noticed that they faulted me for calling the boys not by their real names but 'Charinus' and 'Critias'. Well, on the same grounds they should accuse Gaius Catullus because he used the name 'Lesbia' instead of 'Clodia', and Ticidas similarly because he used 'Perilla' for the actual Metella, and Propertius who writes 'Cynthia' as a cover for Hostia, and Tibullus, because he has Plania in his thoughts but Delia in his poetry.[49]

The identification in 1554 of Catullus's Lesbia as the sister of Clodius Pulcher by Marc-Antoine Muret (1526–1585) gave new impetus to such investigations. Muret himself (who wrote his own Latin love poetry clearly motivated more by his love of ancient poets than by the love of any 'Margaris' – the name he gave to his beloved) in his commentary on Ronsard's *Amours* warned readers that the passionate intensity expressed by love poets ought not to be taken

---

48   See de Beer 2010 for a subtle discussion of this work; see also Charlet 2011.

49   Trans. by C. P. Jones in Apuleius 2017: 32–33.

too literally or seriously.[50] In a more consequential case, Théodore de Bèze (1519–1605) – Latin love poet in his youth, Calvinist theologian and leader in his maturity – faced Catholic and Lutheran opponents who used those youthful fictions as proof of his moral and theological depravity. The 'Candida' he portrayed in his Latin love poems, they said, was his wife; and they gleefully seized upon an epigram about his love for his friend Audebert (*Epig.* 90) supposedly proof of the incontinence of his sexual appetites and of homosexual transgressions. Bèze himself had disowned his erotic epigrams and elegies on his conversion to Calvinism (which occurred shortly after the publication of the *Juvenilia* in 1548), but he was forced to make a case in more general terms against excessively literal-minded readings of those poems:[51]

> Istos bonos viros non pudet quicquid de poëticae Candidae amoribus lusi, (lusi autem certe pleraque, veteres illos imitatus, priusquam etiam per aetatem, quid istud rei esset, intelligerem) ad castissimam et lectissimam foeminam accommodare. Id autem non aliter se habere quam dico, non ii tantum testari possunt quibuscum per id tempus vixi, verum etiam res ipsa declarat: quum nullos unquam liberos ex uxore susceperim, in meis autem illis carminibus, Candidam praegnantem superis commendem: quod tum mihi nimirum illud fictitium argumentum, ut alia subinde multa occurreret.
>
> dedicatory epistle to the second edition of his *Poemata*, 1569

> Those fine men have no shame in applying whatever I wrote unseriously about my love for my poetic creation Candida (and I wrote very many such unserious things, in imitation of the ancients, before I was old enough to understand what it was really all about) to the most chaste and excellent of women [i.e. Bèze's wife]. Proof that I am telling the truth about this can be supplied not only by those with whom I lived at the time, but also by the facts themselves: since I have never had any children from my wife, whereas in my poems I pray for protection of a pregnant Candida: which was obviously a fictional theme that occurred to me then, as many others did later.

Bèze also picked out examples by other contemporary poets to make his case, including the poems by Du Bellay I discussed in the previous section: how was

---

50 See White 2017: 18.

51 Aubert et al. 1980: 88–100; and further on the *querelle des Iuvenilia*, Prescott 1974 and Genton 2007.

it, he asked, that his Catholic critics reserved their opprobrium for Bèze's love poems, and did not apply the same literal standards of interpretation to poems by Catholic authors like Du Bellay, who in one of his epigrams depicts the rape of a nun ("sacrae virginis raptum describit") – indeed they celebrated them!

Looking back on these debates from his sceptical vantage point a century or so later, Pierre Bayle (1647–1706) assessed the validity of the different views. In his *Dictionnaire* article on the Neo-Latin poet Petrus Lotichius Secundus (1528–1560), Bayle digressed on the issue in one his unfailingly entertaining long footnotes (which are more like short essays), considering the different strategies used by love poets and their editors to justify erotic poetry.[52] To a sceptic like Bayle, it seemed ridiculous and childish to attempt to sever the link between love poetry and the real life sexual *mores* of the poet by arguing (as Lotichius had) that the erotic love depicted in his poetry was really just a proxy for divine love. And he was just as dismissive of the vaguely Neo-Platonic argument of Paulus Melissus (1539–1602): Melissus had expounded the principle that the celestial influences that inspire pure love are also the source of poetic inspiration, which explained and justified the propensity of poets to love.[53]

Bayle himself saw no need for such justifications, since (he claimed) poetic love is mostly a fiction. The love that poets describe and perform in their texts is often a mere *jeu d'esprit*, and may have no basis at all in their experience. The intensity of desire we find expressed in love poetry may be just an effect of *imitatio*: poets are always striving to go one better than their models, so they amplify the figures and tropes they have read, and devise new and more forceful ways of saying the same thing.

In support, Bayle used the passage from Bèze quoted above, concluding: "Voyez dans ces dernières paroles un exemple de la conduite des poëtes: ils se donnent des sujets imaginaires, afin d'avoir occasion de débiter quelques traits d'esprit" (Observe in these last words an example of how poets operate: they come up with imaginary subjects, so as to have the opportunity to reel off a few witty conceits).

The Bèze affair cast a long shadow, and in the latter part of the sixteenth century we see both Catholic and Protestant love poets become more circumspect

---

52   Bayle 1697: 387–388.
53   The text to which Bayle refers is a long poem in elegiacs (henceforth "Ad Iohannem Hagium"), addressed by Melissus to Lotichius's biographer Johannes Hagius, which had a separate print publication (Melissus 1583) and then appeared as *Eleg.* 4.2 in his collected poems (Melissus 1586). The poem bears the title "That Love is divinely begotten in humans, which is why it is the most oft-sung subject in the writings of poets" ("Amorem divinitus esse ingeneratum in hominibus, unde Poëtarum scriptis decantatissimus sit") and the subtitle "Defence of Lotichius and of the author" ("Defensio et Lotichii et auctoris"). On this poem see Schäfer 2001 and Descoings 2009; and further below, pp. 73–74.

in the presentation of their poetic love relationships. Two examples of different approaches are furnished by Martial Monier, and Paulus Melissus – who specifically cited the Bèze controversy in defence of his own love poetry.[54]

Ovid's Corinna, widely acknowledged as a fictional creation (and conspicuously unmentioned by Apuleius), provided a model for poets who wished to emphasize the literary ludic dimension of their love poetry and to dodge questions of identification, and allegations of impropriety. (They could also 'take the fifth' by invoking the *lex catulliana*, on which see below pp. 81–88). Martial Monier (b.1548) called his own elegiac mistress 'Corinna', and played repeatedly on the connection to her Ovidian namesake in his elegies and epigrams (1572). He also prefaced the edition of his poems with a lengthy apology, and included, among the numerous dedicatory epigrams that introduce his *Epigrammata*, more than one that insisted on the fictionality of the love poetry: "Why, Monier, do you write of Venus and Venus's little boy? Venus and Venus's boy have nothing to do with you. The fictional representation of Venus that you create is so real that the real one is lesser than your fictive Venus".[55] The general presentation of the poems indicates that some risk was perceived in being taken too literally. This explicit insistence on the fictionality of the love poems seems to have been motivated partly by the fact that the poet was apparently extremely young at the time of their composition, and partly by the general atmosphere in Paris at a time when the publication of love poetry was deemed to require special justification.[56]

The love poetry of Paulus Melissus has itself been subjected to the attentions of modern critics preoccupied with fixing the identity of his beloved 'Rosina': she is sometimes identified with his wife Amilia Jordan, sometimes with a lady in the Elizabethan court, and sometimes with Elizabeth I herself.[57] Melissus addressed the question more than once in his poems; his response is less glib than it appears:

---

54   "Ad Iohannem Hagium", 193–208.
55   "Cur Venerem scribis Moneri Venerisque puellum? / Nil in te est Veneri, nil Veneris puero est. / Sic veram fingis Venerem sub imagine falsa, / Ut sit vera minor quam tua ficta Venus."
56   This had been the argument made by a certain Nicolas Bonyer who had published in Paris 1562 a translation into French of Mantuan's *Contra poetas impudice scribentes*: that in the context of the turmoil caused by the religious conflicts, Mantuan's text needed a revival in order to urge the French poets of the time to turn away from love and other such foolish subjects, and to find other topics more suited to the times. For an analysis of the translation itself, see Bouscharain 2006; and further on Mantuan's *Contra poetas*, see below pp. 84–85.
57   For an overview, see Dana Sutton's introduction to his online edition *Paulus Melissus Schede: The English Poetry (1586)* <http://www.philological.bham.ac.uk/schede/>.

Fortassis et Rosina quae sit
Nostra rogaveris.
Equidem ipsemet (credas velim)
Ignoro. Numquam enim Rosinam
Vidi ego, quam cano
Cecinique, quamque post canam.

"Ad Elisabetham Angliae Reginam", 10–17

Perhaps you will also ask who my Rosina is. Please believe me: even I don't know the answer myself. For I have never seen Rosina, the one whom I sing, whom I have sung and will sing again.

Nos quoque [...]
Speratam numeris fictis cantare ROSINAM,
    Per bis terna fere lustra peracta, iuvat.
Illam ego nec visam, nec posthac forte videndam
    Depereo, miserum tostus amore iecur.

"Ad Iohannem Hagium", 153–7

I too have taken pleasure in singing my longed-for Rosina in fictional strains, throughout these last three decades. I die for her, scorched by love in my miserable guts, though she has never been seen, and perhaps is destined never to be seen in the future.

Although Melissus is in part playing on the elegiac convention of the fictionality of the *puella* (evoking in particular Ovid, who begs readers to give less credence to his depiction of the pseudonymous Corinna in *Am.* 3.12), the point he wants to make is not exactly that his 'Rosina' was merely an invented pretext enabling him to reel off a few witty conceits. Later on he claims that he once saw Rosina's face in a dream, and has yearned for her ever since. His purpose is to make her into the idealized mistress of Petrarchan lyric: an equivalent of Laura, mentioned earlier in the same poem as "once seen" ("visa semel") by Petrarch in a moment that inspired his lasting devotion.

4   Petrarchism

Petrarch was himself a Neo-Latin poet – indeed he was the 'father' of Neo-Latin poetry – but his vernacular poetry is of far greater importance for our study of early modern Latin love poetry than is his Latin. This is partly because of the obvious fact that he wrote much more on the theme of love in Tuscan than he did in Latin; but it is also a general feature of his early modern reception (and indeed of his reception to this day) that his vernacular works enjoyed far greater success and were imitated far more widely than his Latin works.[58]

The presence of Petrarchan elements – stylistic, thematic and structural – in Latin love poetry of the *Quattrocento* is so remarkably pervasive as to be commonplace.[59] Although Landino's elegiac *Xandra* is often viewed as a work of primarily classical inspiration, the programmatic poem *Xandra* 1.2 (as Donatella Coppini has observed) announces the poetic project with a skilful blend of Propertian and Petrarchan elements, the latter even dominating over the former – and the fact of the vernacular presence in a Latin collection "costituisce la più grande novità, perché normale è".[60] The presence of Petrarch in the final version of the *Xandra* is indeed pervasive, ranging from specific instances of allusion or use of Petrarchan motifs, through the description of the beloved and the characterization of the love relationship, to the structuring of the cycle as a chronological sequence. Landino also includes direct translations from Petrarch poems and experimental imitations of Petrarchan forms in Latin (1.7, *Seni senarii ad imitationem Petrarcae*).

Petrarch's love poems in the Tuscan language were themselves thoroughly imbued with his reading of the ancient Latin love poets, so it is unsurprising that Neo-Latin poets found it natural to integrate the vernacular tradition into their classicizing compositions: the two traditions were thoroughly intertwined, not distinct and separate sources of invention. Indeed, in the eyes of Neo-Latin imitators, Petrarch's sonnets could be viewed as a culmination of the ancient traditions of love poetry, a new, improved version of Propertius or Ovid, because they treated erotic themes chastely.[61]

Landino's scholarly interest in Petrarch (he would go on to publish commentaries of Petrarch's *canzoniere* as well as of Dante) disposed him to work this synthesis into his Latin poetry, as part of his efforts to elevate the Tuscan

---

58   On the early modern reception of Petrarch's Latin works compared to his vernacular works, see Hankins 2012. Critical works on early modern Petrarchism which give some attention to Neo-Latin poetry include: Forster 1969; Chines et al. 2006; Enenkel & Papy 2006; Coppini & Feo 2012. Cinti 2006 gives a (rather sketchy) overview of some examples of Petrarchan Latin love poetry beyond Italy.

59   Fantazzi 1996, with particular attention to the love poems of Poliziano.

60   Coppini 2006: 209. See also McLaughlin 1995: 167–171 for an analysis of Landino's *contaminatio* imitation of vernacular Petrarchan and Latin classical sources in the first two books of *Xandra*. A more general account can be found in McNair 2019: 14–27.

61   Landino stated this directly, in his *Proemio al commento dantesco*: see Cardini 1973: 5 and McLaughlin 1995: 171.

literary tradition to the level of the classics and to cement the foundational status of its *Tre Corone* (Dante, Petrarch and Boccaccio).

Landino's integration of Petrarchan elements into his Latin love elegy is more thoroughgoing than any of his immediate predecessors, although their poetry also showed a marked Petrarchan influence too, as we have seen. After Landino we encounter many more love elegy collections whose inspiration is more Petrarchan than elegiac, particularly in – but not limited to – the Florentine context: the *Flametta* of Ugolino Verino (1438–1516); the *Alba* of Naldo Naldi (1436–c.1516) – i.e. book 1 of his *Elegiae*; the *Amorum libellus* of Alessandro Braccesi (1445–1503); and the *Eroticon* of Tito Vespesiano Strozzi (1424–c.1505).

To take one example of the way these poets blended a Petrarchan sensibility and Petrarchan themes with the form and language of Latin love elegy, let us consider the set piece known as the *innamoramento* (the scene of falling in love). Petrarch's *Canz.* 3 ("Era il giorno ch'al sol si scolororo") set the scene of his first encounter with Laura, which famously took place on Good Friday in April 1327. The significance of the date is two-fold: the springtime setting evokes various poetic models, including the mediaeval *Natureingang*; and the religious festival associates the moment with the Christian narrative of world-shattering suffering and redemption.

T. V. Strozzi and Nicodemo Folengo (born *c.*1454) both place at the start of their love elegy books poems that merge the Petrarchan *innamoramento* with the classical elegiac theophany (appearance of the god). Strozzi, for his *innamoramento* (*Eroticon* 1.2; 1.1. in earlier versions), chooses another date in springtime, 23 April, also a religious festival, but more thematically significant in the poem is the fact that it is the day of the *palio di San Giorgio*, a horse race which took place in Ferrara every year.[62] Strozzi nudges the Petrarchan scene in the direction of Ovidian parody: Cupid appears to the poet and, in the manner of Ovid *Am.* 1.1, forces him to love and to write love elegy – although unlike in the Ovidian model, what he is being compelled to reject in favour of elegy is not the higher genre of epic, but merely the idle pleasure of spectating on horse-racing.[63] On one level, the horses could be interpreted as a metonymy for the epic genre – horses sometimes have this association in the ancient *recusationes* – but on another level the poem as a whole is to be read as a reworking

---

[62]   On this poem see Pieper 2010: 59–63 and Mindt 2017: 175–6. See also Beleggia 2006 on the persistence of Petrarchan allusions in the later books of the *Eroticon*.

[63]   "Atque ait, o Iuvenis volucrum mirator equorum / Quod mirere magis, nunc mea dextra dabit" (1.2.19–20) ("And he said, 'Young man, admirer of the swift horses, / now my right hand will give you something to admire more.'").

of its Ovidian elegiac intertexts: not just *Am.* 1.1, but also *Ars Amatoria* 1.135–76 and *Am.* 3.2, where attending horse races is a cover for illicit dalliances.

Folengo, like Strozzi, adopts for his elegiac theophany poem (*Elegiarum liber* 2) a concrete setting evocative of the Petrarchan *innamoramento*: in this case, a wedding taking place on the Nativity of John the Baptist. The poet says he was scorning love, doubting its power. Cupid's chariot appears, leading in chains a group of youths who, to judge from the language that is used to describe their plaints, could even be the ancient elegiac poets themselves:

> Duriciem gemit hic, fastus dolet alter heriles,
>   Ille novi inspectum deflet amantis iter;
> Hunc custos, alium sera coniugis, hunc ferus angit
>   Ianitor aut fallax serva levisque puer;
> Crebra movent aliis duri suspiria patres,
>   Claudicat hic tenero vulnere, at ille gemit.
>   *Elegiarum liber* 2.27–32

One laments his mistress's harshness, another bemoans her disdain, another sees the path of a new lover and weeps; one is pained by a guard, another by a husband's lock, another by a fierce doorkeeper or a deceitful servant girl or a fickle boy; in others hard fathers stir frequent sighs, one limps from a tender wound, another moans.

Cupid corners the poet as he attempts to escape, threatens him, then shoots him, at which point he immediately capitulates and professes his surrender to love. The appearance of the enchained procession of lovers, their utterances marked by pointedly elegiac language, seems to shift the frame of reference away from the initially Petrarchan setting. However the scene of the triumphant Cupid leading prisoners in chains is also a deft blend of Petrarchan and elegiac models: it evokes Petrarch's *Triumph of Love*, but in its language foregrounds the elegiac intertexts, Ovid *Amores* 1.2.23–52 and Propertius 3.1.11–12.

There is certainly some truth to Ludwig's passing remark that Neo-Latin elegy can be considered "as the humanistic answer to Petrarch's vernacular love poetry", and that "elegy was discovered as the Latin equivalent of the Italian sonnet".[64] Many Neo-Latin elegies resemble sonnets in length, structure and conceit. Throughout the period numerous Neo-Latin authors translated poems from the *Canzoniere* into Latin, and some integrated their translations into their own books of love poems. Sonnets by Petrarch and his imitators in

---

64   Ludwig 1976: 173.

vernacular languages were often translated into Latin elegiacs, and in some cases their translators clearly wished to highlight the compatibility of the sonnet form with the Latin genre of love elegy. Two examples from the latter part of the sixteenth century will suffice to give a sense of how this worked. Both the obscure French poet Nicolas Brizard (1520–1565) and the celebrated Dutch poet Janus Dousa (1545–1604) composed Latin love elegy collections incorporating translations from Petrarch. Brizard published in 1556 a collection of *Elegiae amatoriae* containing 16 short love elegies addressed to his beloved, a Bruxelloise wool-worker called 'Flora'. No less than four of these elegies are marked as translations from Petrarch, all adjusted to address Brizard's Flora and more or less smoothly integrated into his own elegiac sequence.[65] When Janus Dousa's collected poems were published in 1609, the editor Petrus Scriverius attached to Dousa's love elegy collection *Cupidinum libri duo* a number of Dousa's translations of sonnets into Latin elegiacs, which show Dousa integrating vernacular traditions of love poetry into his classicizing elegiac discourse. Among them were two Petrarch translations, again adjusted to align with the elegiac situation of the *Cupidines*, addressed to a beloved named 'Ida'.[66]

Since both poets translated *Canzoniere* 132 ("S'amor non è, che dunque è quel ch'io sento?") – a very popular choice among Neo-Latin poets because it typified that feature of the Petrarchan style that most appealed to them, the oxymoronic formulation[67] – a comparison of the two efforts is in order. Brizard's version is titled "De vultu Florae suae" and begins: "sentio visceribus quod me titillat in imis, / Hoc faciunt vultus Belgica Nympha tui". It is precisely half the length of Dousa's, which runs to 48 elegiac lines: "Esse quid hoc dicam quod sentio? quid, nisi amorem?". Both Dousa and Brizard personalize their versions of Petrarch, inserting the name of their elegiac *puella* into the composition: Ida in the case of Dousa, Flora in Brizard's case.

Despite the difference in length, Dousa's versions of specific lines from Petrarch are in fact closer to the original than Brizard's, although Dousa has also worked to amplify the Petrarchan images and formulations, and to push them further into alignment with the elegiac discourse. For example, in

---

65   The poems are: "De ore eiusdem ad Cupidinem: ex Petrarcha. *Stiamo Amor a veder*" (*Canz.* 192); "Ad Floram suam, quibus modis eius causa crucietur. Ex Fr. Petrarcha. *Pace non trovo.*" (134); "De vultu Florae suae. Ex Fr. Petrarcha. *S'amor non è, che dunque è*" (132); "Ad Floram, Quibus laqueis et artibus amor Poetam irretivit. Ex Fr. Petrar. *Amor m'ha posto, come segno*" (133).

66   "Elegia I. Ex Rhythmis Italicis Francisci Petrarchae" (132: *S'amor non è, che dunque è quel ch'io sento?*); and "Elegia II. Ex eodem" (129: *Di pensier in pensier, di monte in monte*).

67   On the popularity of this sonnet, see Forster 1969: 4–8.

translating the lines "O viva morte, o dilectoso male, come puoi tanto in me, s'io no 'l consento?", Dousa writes:

O gratum tormentum, o vivae mortis imago,
    Unde in me tantum iuris, inique, tibi:
Tantum unde imperii est Puer audacissime, si non
    Quae facis, haec pariter me cupiente facis?
Sed cupiente facis me scilicet omnia, et ipse
    Conqueror immerito de feritate tua.
Sic mecum pugno assidue sic versat in orbem,
    Meque animi captum ludificatur Amor.
Ipsa mihi est odio pax, nec tamen aequa gerundi
    Arma potestatem mi semel Ida facit.
Quo vero arma mihi, quem (si fas dicere, sed fas)
    Illa vel armatum vincere nuda potest?[68]

O pleasurable torment, o image of living death, whence comes the so great influence you unjustly have over me? Whence comes your so great power, you very presumptuous boy, if what you do, you do not equally do when I desire it? But you do of course do it all when I desire it, and I complain unfairly of your savagery. Thus do I battle with myself constantly, and thus Amor has me going in circles, and makes a mockery of me, a prisoner of my heart. Peace itself is hateful to me, but neither has Ida once given me the opportunity of being armed for a fair fight. But armed to what end, if she can – I hesitate to say it – if she can, unclothed, defeat me even in full armour?

A fairly precise translation of the Italian lines in the first couplet leads into an expansive passage that is elegiac more than it is Petrarchan: Dousa introduces the tropes of the *imperium* of Amor and *militia amoris*, but adjusts them sufficiently to the Petrarchan context of paradoxical self-division and mental confusion that the transition is not jarring. By the time Dousa is writing, the themes and images of Petrarchism and classical elegy have become so intertwined in Neo-Latin love poetry that it does not seem at all unusual to give Petrarch in translation all the appearance of a Latin love elegist.

Brizard's version of the lines is looser, not to say repetitious and clumsy, but he does not attempt anything like the expansive departures of Dousa.

---

68   Dousa 1609: 565–6.

Tristes delitias, certamque in funere vitam!
   Cur in me tantum me renuente potes?
Delitiae nimium, nimium mors in mea possunt
   Funera [...][69]

Sorrowful delights, a life fixed on death! Why do you have such great power over me, when I refuse it? Delights have too much power, death has too much power to bring about my ruin [...]

Rather, Brizard's effort to integrate the Petrarchan sonnet into his own elegiac sequence is in the framing: the opening couplet (not in the original) specifies that his disturbance is caused by the sight of Flora, and particularizes Petrarch's "amor" as the elegiac "puer ... facibus, telisque instructus et arcu".

5   Mediaeval Presences

The presence of 'mediaevalisms' in early modern literature and art has become a focus of scholarship in recent years.[70] This can be seen from one angle as a justified reaction against a set of tacit assumptions that had coloured much of the older criticism, amounting to an unreflective acceptance of the view of themselves that Renaissance humanists strove to present to the world: that their project to revivify classical forms entailed a wholesale rejection of all that was mediaeval.

We have already touched on the importance of the *Tre Corone* of Dante, Petrarch and Boccaccio for the Italian Neo-Latin love poetry of the fifteenth century. The moods and general attitudes of much of this early humanist poetry were also informed by other late mediaeval vernacular and Latin traditions – the carnivalesque world of the *fabliaux* and *novelle*, and the satirical and bawdy strains of the goliardic poets and the comedies.[71] The *fin amors* tradition in romance and in the lyrics of the troubadours and the *stilnovisti* has been mentioned already. In general we are dealing here with more or less indirect inflections of theme and mood, and submerged memories of particular poetic formulations and images. Much work remains to be done on instances of more direct and sustained engagements with mediaeval traditions.

---

69   Brizard 1556: 49v–50r.
70   See for example Eisenbichler 2009 and, especially, Montoya et al. 2010.
71   See Parker's comments in Beccadelli 2010: xxiv–xxvi.

In an article on mediaeval elements in Neo-Latin love poetry of the early *Quattrocento* (Marrasio, Landino and Strozzi), Christoph Pieper rightly observes that humanist poets often wished to highlight their indebtedness to the classical models and to disavow mediaeval influences. Where poets drew upon mediaeval sources (and they did – particularly in moments of self-consciousness about poetic tradition), they tended to conceal, or at least not to highlight, these influences.[72] Deliberate suppression or concealment is one possible explanation for the low visibility of mediaeval elements in Neo-Latin love poetry, even where they are present. Another is the fact that the traditions were so thoroughly intertwined that they are difficult to disentangle: as Pieper observes, mediaeval love poetry had itself absorbed and transformed themes and formulations from classical love poetry, which had in turn been absorbed into Petrarchism.[73]

There are also other ways to account for it. If the classical was absorbed into the mediaeval, the mediaeval could also be absorbed into the classical. To explain what I mean by this, I will take the example of the theme known as the *descriptio pulchritudinis*. The elements of this poetic set-piece, a type of *blason* or systematic description of feminine physical beauty, were established in late antiquity and in the Middle Ages: golden hair, black, arched eyebrows, eyes like stars, red lips. This grouping of elements is found quite often in Neo-Latin love poetry, and in some cases it is likely that the source is the mediaeval tradition as codified in works like the *Poetria nova* of Geoffrey of Vinsauf and the *Ars versificatoria* of Matthew of Vendôme.[74] But later Neo-Latin poets could find these elements in 'classical' sources, too.

When Konrad Celtis (1459–1508) composed his *Amorum libri quattuor* (print publication 1502), he included a description of the beauty of his beloved Hasilina with the elements listed above (*Am.* 1.8.12–15). Jörg Robert has plausibly argued that Celtis drew this description from a poem by the sixth-century elegist Maximianus, probably via later mediaeval sources such as the ones named above (since the "star-like eyes" are not present in Maximianus, but are in the mediaeval reformulations), all the while studiously concealing his non-classical sources.[75] But Celtis could actually have pointed to a 'classical'

---

72   Pieper 2010.

73   Pieper 2010: 56 also makes a different – not entirely convincing – argument in relation to Marrasio: that he "deliberately contrasted [the mediaeval models] with the ancient models to highlight his conscious choice for a new beginning."

74   For example *Angelinetum* 2.12–18 (and 3.13–14), discussed by Pieper 2010: 52–6 and by Coppini 2000 (with fuller discussion of other examples in Neo-Latin love elegy).

75   Robert 2003: 340–2; see also Gärtner 2015 for Celtis's imitation of Maximianus more generally.

source for all of the elements of his *descriptio*: Gaius Cornelius Gallus. In 1502, the elegiac corpus of Maximianus, together with a poem in accentual hendecasyllabics known as the *Carmen ad Lydiam* ("Lydia bella puella candida"), was attributed in print to the classical elegist Gallus, a false attribution which was to have a long and consequential afterlife.[76]

> Lydia bella puella, candida,
> Quae bene superas lac et lilium
> Albamque simul rosam rubidam,
> Aut expolitum ebur Indicum,
> Pande, puella, pande capillulos
> Flavos, lucentes ut aurum nitidum.
> Pande, puella, collum candidum
> Productum bene candidis humeris.
> Pande, puella, stellatos oculos
> Flexaque super nigra cilia.
> Pande, puella, genas roseas,
> Perfusas rubro purpuræ Tyriae.
> Porrige labra, labra corallina,
> Da columbatim mitia basia.
>
> *Carmen ad Lydiam* 1–14

Lydia, bright and beautiful, surpassing milk and the lily, and the rose both white and red, or polished Indian ivory. Show me, my girl, show me your blond hair, that shines like bright gold. Show me, my girl, show me your white neck, extending finely from your white shoulders. Show me, my girl, your starry eyes, and your curved black eyebrows. Show me, my girl, your rosy cheeks, suffused with the blush of Tyrian purple. Offer your lips, your coral-red lips; give me soft kisses like a dove.

The "starry eyes", absent from Maximianus (now 'Gallus') *Eleg.* 1.89–100, are present and correct in *Carmen ad Lydiam* 9 (now by the same author). Celtis may well have known these poems as the work of Gallus, either through the 1502 print edition or in the fifteenth-century manuscripts in which the attribution first appeared. There would thus have been no need for Celtis to conceal his borrowings from non-classical sources, since the sources themselves had been reimagined as genuine works of classical antiquity.

---

[76]   On Renaissance imitations of the *Carmen ad Lydiam*, see White 2019: 28; Fantazzi 1996: 136.

6 Virgilian Pastoral and Horatian Lyric

Neo-Latin love poets seeking models in Augustan poetry were not, of course, limited to the genre of Roman love elegy: both Virgil and Horace wrote love poetry, the former in the pastoral genre and the latter as a lyric poet. Both were widely imitated in poetry written in those genres and in others.

At the start of the seventeenth century it was common knowledge that love is the most traditional subject of the pastoral genre – this, at least, was the view expressed by Daniel Heinsius (1580–1655) in a letter to Constantijn Huygen: "nemo quoque nescit [...] materiam eorum [i.e. Idyllorum sive Eclogarum] antiquissimam amores esse".[77] But it had not always been obvious to all that Virgilian pastoral should be viewed primarily as 'love poetry'. Some imitators did their best to downplay pastoral's erotic themes – Petrarch, for example, in his *Bucolica* barely touched on them – and almost all suppressed the specifically homosexual elements, most notoriously present in Virgil's second *Eclogue*. The *Adulescentia* of Mantuan (Baptista Spagnuoli Mantuanus, 1447–1516), a hugely influential collection, did re-establish love as a central theme of pastoral, and, as Lee Piepho showed, some of its early publishers used its eroticism to promote their editions.[78] (They knew that sex sells, even for an author as profoundly unsexy as Mantuan.) Some editors and commentators, particularly those who were educators – since Mantuan quickly became a standard school author – expressed a degree of uneasiness about the prominence of the love theme in the *Adulescentia*, but they were comforted by the clarity with which the poet distinguished *honestus amor* from illicit and disruptive desire, and by the forcefulness of his explicit misogyny. Some editions included in addition to the ten eclogues of the *Adulescentia* Mantuan's poem *Elegia contra amorem* (Elegy against love), a fact which they advertised on their title pages.[79]

Many of the Neo-Latin poets I have mentioned so far in the context of love elegy also composed pastoral collections. In fifteenth-century Italy, when Virgilian pastoral was a very widely practiced Neo-Latin genre, Aeneas Silvius Piccolomini, Naldo Naldi, Tito Vespesiano Strozzi and Giovanni Pontano all wrote eclogues alongside their love elegies. Those collections were not primarily erotic in their thematic focus, but from the first decades of the sixteenth century we see the development of new, non-Virgilian, forms of Neo-Latin pastoral whose main theme was love.

---

77 Quoted by Heckel 2014: 15.
78 Piepho 1989: 17.
79 Piepho 2006: 65.

The form known as the *lusus pastoralis* is closely associated with two poets, Andrea Navagero (1483–1529) and Marcantonio Flaminio (1498–1550). These are shorter non-hexametric poems (which have been labelled 'pastoral epigrams') combining bucolic settings and characters with language and themes borrowed from other genres, and drawing on a range of models including epigrams from the Greek Anthology, the poems of the Roman love elegists and Catullus, and Petrarchan sonnets.

Navagero's *Lusus* (first published in print in 1530, after his death)[80] consists of a handful of pastoral poems of the Virgilian type together with around thirty shorter poems in elegiacs, hendecasyllables and other metres. The love theme dominates in a grouping of poems in which the persona laments, in Catullan style, his unrequited love for one 'Hyella' (a name that would recur in Flaminio's *lusus*), and for various other women. This collection was widely read and imitated, and was particularly admired by Joachim Du Bellay, whose *Divers jeux rustiques* (1558) contains several French versions of poems by Navagero.

Flaminio's 'Hyella cycle' (composed 1539–40 and published as book 4 of his *Carmina*) combines pastoral settings with the language and themes of love poetry in varied metrical forms to tell the story of the tragic love of 'Iolas' and 'Hyella'. Given the narrative continuity linking the poems in the collection, it has been called both a "*canzoniere pastorale*", and a "pastoral romance" comparable to Sannazaro's *Arcadia* "but without the prose links".[81] In the first poem in the sequence, composed in an epodic metre (iambic trimeters followed by dimeters), the Muse of Catullus is invoked as the presiding spirit for this hybrid genre:

> O quae venusta Sirmionis litora
> Colis, Catulli candida
> Musa, et beatam citrii silvam doces
> Pulchram sonare Lesbiam,
> En nos Taburni in valle florida tibi
> Aram virenti e caespite,
> Et terna melle, terna lacte ponimus
> Spumante plena cymbia,
> Et te vocamus voce supplici, dea,
> Ad sacra parva, sed pia,
> Vt nostram Hyellam fistula dulci canas;
> Qua nulla rure pulchrior

---

80   On which see Nichols 1998.
81   Ferroni 2012: 248–262; Maddison 1965: 98.

Vixit, nec ulla vivet ullo tempore
Cani puella dignior.

You who dwell by the charming shores of Sirmio, bright Muse of Catullus, and teach the happy citrus grove to sing beautiful Lesbia, see how I in the florid vale of Taburno offer you an altar made of green turf and cups filled, three with honey and three with foaming milk, and call you in prayer, goddess, to accept my meagre yet pious offerings, that you sing my Hyella to the accompaniment of the sweet reed-pipe, for none more beautiful than her has ever lived in any countryside, and no girl will ever live at any time more worthy of being sung.

The Catullan influence on the poems in this collection is, in fact, from a formal and stylistic point of view less obvious than it is for Navagero's *Lusus* (other than in terms of its polymetric variety). What Flaminio seems to have had in mind were the general poetic qualities of simplicity and *suavitas*, which he associated primarily with Catullus, and wanted to achieve in this collection. The poetry draws on a wide range of classical and vernacular models, not the least of which is the vernacular Petrarchan tradition, including the *Canzoniere* of Bembo, and the *Arcadia* of Jacopo Sannazaro (1458–1530).[82]

Sannazaro's reinvention of pastoral, *Arcadia* (1504), established love as a fundamental part of the genre in a way that was to have a lasting influence on its later development. The *Arcadia* was written in the vernacular, but among Sannazaro's Latin poems the *Eclogae piscatoriae* also gives examples of hexameter pastoral with erotic themes. In fact it depicts a coastal (not pastoral) landscape populated by fishermen singing their unhappy and happy loves in the manner of Virgilian and Theocritean lovers.[83] His second eclogue, for example, which has the fisherman Lycon singing an erotic lament for his unrelenting lover Galatea, evokes Virgil *Ecl.* 2, then in the following passage (in which Lycon fantasizes about faraway travels to forget his love, but comes to the realization that love conquers all) clearly recalls Virgil, *Ecl.* 10.64–69:

Heu quid agam? Externas trans pontum quaerere terras
Iam pridem est animus, quod numquam navita, numquam
Piscator veniat; fors illic nostra licebit

---

82 Comiati 2018: 197–202.

83 For the *Eclogae Piscatoriae* see the editions of Mustard (Sannazaro 1914), Martini (Sannazaro 1995) and Putnam (Sannazaro 2009); and Fredericksen 2014, Czapla 2006 (on *Ecl. Pisc.* 2 in particular).

Fata queri. Boreae extremo damnata sub axe
Stagna petam et rigidis numquam non cana pruinis
An Libyae rapidas Austrique tepentis harenas,
Et videam nigros populos Solemque propinquum?
Quid loquor infelix? An non per saxa, per ignes,
Quo me cumque pedes ducent, mens aegra sequetur?
Vitantur venti, pluviae vitantur et aestus,
Non vitatur amor; mecum tumuletur oportet.

Alas, what shall I do? It has long since been my thought to seek out for-
eign lands across the sea, never reached by a sailor, never by a fisherman. There chance will allow me to lament my fate. Shall I go in search of
sluggish waters, consigned beneath the farthest pole of Boreas, eternally
white with stiffening chill, or shall I view the scorching sands of Libya
and of the searing Auster, and dark-skinned races and the nearby Sun?
What am I saying, in my misfortune? Through rocks, through flames –
wherever my feet take me – won't my troubled mind follow? Winds can
be avoided, rains and sweltering heat avoided, but love is not avoidable.
It should go to my grave with me.[84]

That Sannazaro's Lycon here sounds very much like an elegiac lover struggling
to be free of himself and fantasizing about escape to far-off lands is no acci-
dent: the model for this pastoral figure is Virgil's Gallus, a transplant from the
elegiac to the pastoral landscape. In Virgil's *Ecl.* 10 the presence of the elegist
Gallus might seem to the modern reader a jarring instance of genre cross-over,
but ancient elegy itself (despite its credentials as an urban genre) frequently
invoked the world of pastoral. In the poetry of Tibullus in particular, pastoral
landscapes are a pervasive presence in the dream-life of the elegiac persona.
Sometimes these rustic visions serve as a foil or contrast for elegiac disillu-
sionment (with the supposedly happy and carefree love of pastoral being a
counterpoint to elegiac lament), and sometimes they simply live in the space
of fantasy and daydream – eroticism in the subjunctive mood. Neo-Latin poets
recognized the complementarity of the two genres and they frequently incor-
porated pastoral scenes and landscapes into their elegiac books, and brought
elegiac moods and language into hexameter pastoral.

Later in the period we find Neo-Latin collections of pastoral poems presented primarily as love poetry ('amores'). A good example, with a recent modern edition is the *Lalage sive Amores Pastorales* (1613) of Floris van Schoonhoven

---

84   Sannazaro 2009: 116–117. Translation by Michael C. J. Putnam.

(1594–1648).[85] Van Schoonhoven also wrote a book of hexametric *Bucolica* of the Virgilian type, but his *Lalage* is clearly in the lineage of the *lusus pastorales* of Navagero and Flaminio. It consists of forty short lyrics in various metres written in the person of a shepherd, Daphnis, who woos his beloved Lalage, eventually succeeds in winning her, and then has to mourn her death. The sequence is followed by two poems in elegiacs which clearly belong to the genre of love elegy and evoke Tibullus in particular – a demonstration of how Neo-Latin poets aligned the two genres, or at least set them side by side.

We also see first-person love elegy collections being inflected by the generic characteristics of the *lusus pastoralis*. Adriaan Reland's *Galatea: Lusus poeticus* (1701)[86] signals an affinity with the latter by its title, although the collection itself, which consists of 13 poems in elegiacs, is very clearly a Latin love elegy book and not a pastoral one. This Galatea is not a bucolic nymph or shepherdess but an elegiac *puella* – albeit a rather distant and chaste one. Reland's use of the designation *lusus* in his title (previously rare in titles of Neo-Latin love elegy collections, but popularized by him and subsequently taken up by several others)[87] is partly there to mark the poems as the product of youthful literary experimentation. But it also unmistakeably evokes the model of Navagero; and the settings of the elegies (natural, non-urban environments) and indeed the underpinning narrative structure (a tight chronological sequence culminating in the death of the beloved) indicate a merging of the conventions of elegiac and pastoral love.

Rustic settings joined with amatory themes appeared frequently, too, in Horatian lyric, and poets like Flaminio drew extensively on Horace's *Odes*. Horace was of course universally admired among humanists, but perhaps more as theorist, moralist or stately lyricist than as a love poet.[88] Horace's love poetry has sometimes been viewed as detached and passionless, but the distancing effect operative in Horatian lyric – which often sees the persona looking back to a time of love now in the past, or looking forward to a future when love will be lost, as an impetus to live the present moment – very much appealed to Renaissance sensibilities. One ode by Flaminio, composed early in his career, provides a fine example of the dominant styles and moods of this type of poetry:

---

85   Heckel 2014.
86   On which see Sacré 2021.
87   Sacré 2021: 246–8.
88   Recent collective publications on the Renaissance reception of Horace with chapters on Neo-Latin poetry: Dauvois et al. 2019; Laureys et al. 2020.

Jam ver floricomum, POSTHUME, verticem
Profert puniceo Chloridis ex sinu,
Jam pellunt Zephyri frigus, et horrida
Tellus exuitur nives.

Cantantes Hadriae marmora navitae
Audent velivolis currere puppibus:
Nec tendens avidis retia piscibus
Hibernas metuit minas

Sardus: jam virides gramina vestiunt
Campos, et tumidis palmes agit graves
Gemmas corticibus: jam volucres suis
Mulcent aëra cantibus.
[...]
Sed curae, heu! miseri sunt animi dapes,
Sed cordis lacrimae pocula, sed quies
Confectum rigidae corpus humi jacens,
Sed carmen mihi flebiles

Questus, et dominae nomina: sic mihi
Numquam veris eunt tempora: sic mihi
Soles non ahquo tempore candidi:
Sic mi perpetua est hiems.

Now, Posthumus, spring raises his flowery locks
From Chloris' rosy bosom, and zephyrs
Drive the cold away, and shaggy
Earth shakes off the snow.

And singing sailors dare skim with their sails
On the polished marble of the Adriatic,
And the Sardinian spreads his nets for the eager
Fish with no fear for the threats

Of winter. Now grass clothes the green
Fields and big buds swell the vine
Shoot's skin. Now birds soften the air
With their songs.
[....]

But, alas, my wretched mind feasts on anxiety
And my heart drinks tears and my rest is a worn-out
Body lying on the iron earth,
And my song is tearful

Lament and the name of my mistress. So
I will never know spring, so the sun will never
Shine bright for me. So, for me, winter
Is without end.[89]

Flaminio here combines echoes of odes of Horace on themes of lost love and the melancholy of springtime (Horace *Carm.* 1.5; 3.9; 4.7) with imitations of Petrarch and Ovid. The overall impression is Horatian, but the ending of the poem moves away from the wry sadness that often characterizes Horace's love poetry to build to a climax of much greater emotional intensity, where the Petrarchan model comes to the fore (*Canz.* 310, "Zephiro torna, e 'l bel tempo rimena").[90]

It was common for Neo-Latin love poetry collections whose dominant genre identity was elegiac or epigrammatic to incorporate compositions in Horatian metres. The *Iulia* of Francesco Ottaviano Cleofilo (1447–1490) is exemplary of the promiscuity with poetic models that characterized the Neo-Latin love poetry book, since it is essentially a Latin love elegy collection written not in elegiacs but in Horatian metres.[91] At times the poems appear merely to be transpositions of the language and themes of love elegy to lyric metrical forms; but the Horatian sensibility is also strongly evident in poems like the following:

Laetare, cordis dimidium mei,
laetare, velox namque fugit aetas.
    En curva iam repet senectus
        instabili tremebunda gressu.

Expelle curas cantibus et sono,
innecte serto tempora myrteo,
    neu sperne fumosum falernum,
        neu tacitis venerem tenebris.

---

89   Text and translation in Maddison 1965: 17–18.
90   For the Petrarchan model, see Comiati 2018: 193–4.
91   De Nichilo 1999, and the edition: Cleofilo 2003.

Dum fata currunt, dum sinit Atropos,
neu perde vitae laetitiam brevem.
   Felix malignos qui dolores
      pectoribus didicit fugare![92]
    Iulia 8

Be glad, my heart's other half, be glad, for time flies swiftly. Soon crooked
old age will creep up shakily on faltering steps. Dispel your cares with
music and song, bind your temples with a myrtle garland, and spurn not
the smoky Falernian, spurn not lovemaking in the silent dark. While the
Fates run on, as long as Atropos permits, waste not the brief joy of life.
Happy the one who has learned in his heart to chase away malign sorrows!

7   Greek Models

Jean Salmon Macrin (1490–1557) liked to characterize himself as the French
Horace. Just as Horace had foregrounded his Greek lyric models, and claimed
to have been the first to have attempted Greek forms in Latin (*Carm.* 3.30.13–14),
so Salmon Macrin was keen to emphasize that his models were not only Roman:

Impune nam si vera faterier
citraque nobis invidiam licet,
   magna ipse primus quem probarit
   Gallia tempus ad hoc poetam,

primus puellae tinnula Lesbiae
qui plectra sumpsi et Pindaricum melos
   non ante vulgata per urbes
   Pictonicas fide publicavi.
    Carmina 1.31.41–48

For if I might speak the truth freely and without fear of envy, I myself
am the first whom great France has so far approved a poet; I, first, took
up the tinkling lyre of the Lesbian girl [i.e. Sappho], and I, first, revealed
to the people Pindaric strains played on the lyre not yet known throughout Poitevin cities.

---

92   For an analysis of the poetic intertexts, see De Nichilo 1999: 282–5.

At a time when Greek learning was still relatively uncommon even among erudite humanists, this claim was, on the surface of it, an audacious one. The lesser claim, that Salmon Macrin was the first in France to write books of Latin odes in the style of Horace, has sometimes been endorsed by critics – though it is not quite true, as Petrus Burrus (1430–1507) had done so some decades earlier. The claim to be writing in imitation of Sappho and Pindar must also be taken lightly. Neo-Latin love poets habitually mentioned Greek models, often because the Roman models they were really imitating themselves did so. It is not uncommon to find in Neo-Latin love elegy, for example, claims to be following in the footsteps of Callimachus and Philetas and Mimnermus. In many cases the authors had not read these poets in Greek (or could not have done so, since the relevant works were not extant), but had found their names in Propertius or in the commentaries. Salmon Macrin, for his part, certainly did know Greek: he had studied it in Paris under the famous Italian Hellenist Girolamo Aleandro (1480–1542). Pindar could be read in the Aldine edition of 1513, but the surviving fragments of Sappho would not be gathered for print publication until the 1550s and 1560s.[93] Salmon Macrin's mention of Pindar here is non-specific and refers to a generalized Pindaric style – elevated, powerful, audacious – as described by Horace (*Carm.* 4.2). The allusion to Sappho evokes Catullus: Macrin describes the "tinkling plectrum" of Sappho using the Catullan word "tinnula", which recalls the "high-pitched voice" of Hymen in Catullus's *epithalamium* (61.13). This is, then, a kind of double-identification of a sort typical among Neo-Latin poets: its point is to fashion a lineage of poets that follows the trajectory of the *translatio studii*, from Greece to Rome and then to modern Europe, in this case France, "magna Gallia".

Another Greek source mentioned by Salmon Macrin in his *Carmina* was Anacreon. Writing before Estienne's edition of the *Anacreontea* (on which see below), a poet like Salmon Macrin would have known Anacreon via testimonies and a couple of epigrams in the Greek Anthology: that is, in the *Anthologia Planudea* – the Anthology of Planudes – which had several print editions dating from 1494 onwards. The major importance of the Greek Anthology as a source of inspiration for Neo-Latin love poetry has been long recognized, ever since the foundational works of James Hutton on the subject.[94] Erotic epigrams from the Anthology served as models for translation or imitation by numerous Neo-Latin poets, and were particularly popular sources of inspiration in the Latin poetry of France and the Low Countries. Johannes Secundus drew on them for his *Basia*, and Lyon poets like Nicolas Bourbon (1503–1550) and

93   Michelakis 2009.
94   Hutton 1935 and Hutton 1946; and for a concise overview consult Haynes 2007.

Gilbert Ducher (b.1490) produced numerous imitations. Important intermediaries were the Latin translations of Andrea Alciato (1492–1550), and, particularly for the erotic epigrams, the *Erotopaignion* (1512) of Girolamo Angeriano (d.1535), which included around thirty Latin translations and adaptations of erotic epigrams from the Anthology. To pick out one example, of *Gr. Anth.* v.74 ("πέμπω σοι, Ῥοδόκλεια, τόδε στέφος ...": "I send you this garland, Rhodoclea ...") we find Latin versions by Angeriano, Marullus, Bourbon and around forty others identified by Hutton. I quote the version of Bourbon, which is clearly influenced by the phrasing of Angeriano:

> Ad puellam
> Accipe multiplici contextam flore corollam,
>   Quam feci digitis dulcis amica meis:
> Accipe, verum istud sibi quid velit accipe donum,
>   Ut pereunt flores, sic tua forma perit.

> To his girlfriend
> Take this garland woven from various flowers, which I made, sweet love, with my own hands: take it, but take note of what this gift signifies: as flowers perish, so too does your beauty.

The collection of poems known as the *Carmina Anacreontea*, consisting of epigrams written in imitation of Anacreon but presented as being by him, became an important source for Neo-Latin poetry in the mid-sixteenth century after its publication by Henri Estienne (c.1531–1598).[95] Estienne's 1554 edition had an immediate impact, aided by the Latin translations of Estienne himself, and of Elie André who issued the first complete translation shortly after the appearance of the Greek *princeps*. It was particularly influential on French poetry, specifically on Pierre de Ronsard and the group of poets known as the Pléiade; Remy Belleau translated it into French in 1556.[96] Johannes Secundus, who had (before Estienne's edition) included a poem in hemiambic metre in his *Basia* (*Basium* 8), seems to have originated an association between Anacreontic and Catullan poetry, which had a long-lasting influence on Neo-Latin and vernacular imitators.[97]

Neo-Latin poets writing 'Anacreontics' produced some of the most unusual and flamboyant love poetry of the period. Not all Anacreontics were love

---

95   See Rosenmeyer 1992: 231–233 and, especially, Tilg 2014.
96   O'Brien 1995; Rosenmeyer 2002.
97   Tilg 2014: 168–171.

poems, but Caspar von Barth (1587–1658), "the most prolific writer of Latin Anacreontics ever",[98] made amatory themes the main focus of his poetry in this mode (of which he produced no less than fifteen books), He used the Anacreontic form to write love poetry liberally seasoned with Catullan-elegiac and Petrarchan motifs. The most eye-catching features of these poems are the polysyllabic neologisms, the manic repetitions and extravagant contortions of syntax (all very quotable but basically untranslatable), but there are also poems in which a simplicity of expression combines memorably with arresting imagery:

> Ego in tuis ocellis
> Oculis meis Amorem
> Vidi, nitens Neaera:
> Hoc pulpitum est Amoris,
> Ille inde dictat, et me
> Iubet notare dicta
> Papyrum in elegantem.
> Rosillus et Neaera,
> Neaera cum Rosillo
> Duo sunt Amoris haedi,
> Duae Columbulae, ah me,
> Duo non sed una et unus.

I in your eyes, with my own eyes, have seen Love, bright Neaera: this is the pulpit of Love, from which he pronounces, and commands me to take down his dictation on elegant papyrus. Rosillus and Neaera, Neaera with Rosillus, are two of Love's kids, two little doves, ah me, not two, but one and one.

Long before Barth, Julius Caesar Scaliger (1484–1558) had been conducting his own experiments with Anacreontic form. Whereas most Neo-Latin poets composed their Anacreontics in the hemiambic and anaclastic metres, Scaliger varies the metrical form with such a degree of irregularity that his compositions read almost like free verse.[99] Scaliger justifies his experiment by quoting Horace's mention of Anacreon's "unworked metre" (*Epodes* 14.12), and associating metrical freedom with the uninhibited expression necessary for a poet writing of the unbounded emotions of love:

---

98   Tilg 2014: 170.
99   Tilg: 2014: 172–5.

Age comites Lyaei
Solvite iugum Camoenis,
Ut amore liberali
Repetamus illa prisca
Concinendi mysteria:
Nec pes cohibeat modos
Qui citatur ad choreas.
Satis inclyti Lyaei est
Animus calore vinctus.
Tetrica hinc facesse Musa.
Claudicare mi iucundum
Titubante gressu fari.
Sat servivimus, sed non sat
Lusimus, ludamus ergo,
Cantillemus et bibamus
Basiemus basiemur.
Precio libertas nullo
Venditur.

Come, companions of Bacchus the Loosener, unfasten the Muses from the yoke, so that we may revive with free love those ancient mysteries of song: no metrical foot should constrain the rhythm; the foot is compelled to dance. It is enough that the mind is bound with the heat of glorious Bacchus. Begone from here, gloomy Muse. My pleasure is to limp, to speak with reeling steps. We have been enslaved enough, but we have not played enough, so let us play, let's sing and drink, let's kiss and be kissed. Freedom is not for sale at any price.

J. C. Scaliger was a pretty idiosyncratic critic and writer, but it was by no means a notion unique to him that Greek erotic poetry offered imitators a looseness and freedom of expression and a licence with form and metre unavailable in the classical Roman models. The idea that the conventional metrical forms of classical Latin poetry might be unsuited to love because they constrained the expression of boundless emotion came up in the works of other love poets too.

At the start of the seventeenth century, Daniel Heinsius was the author of an intriguing project to make Latin love elegy *more Greek*. Heinsius wrote a number of books of Latin love elegy, the most interesting of which is the one he called *Monobiblos sive Elegiarum liber singularis* (1603; substantially altered in several later editions). In the dedication of that work to Scriverius, Heinsius says he separated out his *Monobiblos* from his main elegiac collection because he saw it as an experimental attempt to work a 'Greek' style into Latin love poetry. His explanation is worth quoting at length:

> Inventiones vagas, liberas, lascivas, solutas, amoenas, et, ut uno verbo absolvam, Graecas, quae felicitate sua, et motuum celeritate; suavitate denique et lepore Romanos terrere solent, hac tanquam fasce quodam, comprehendi. [...] Idem in Graecorum nonnullis inaffectatae elegantiae affectator ille Catullus noster praestitit et in primo libro suo maxime Umber, qui quotiescunque aliquid supra Romanos audet, Callimachum se vocat. Excepta tamen una et altera Elegia, minus amoenitati se dedit; minusque, sive certo iudicio, sive alias naturae suasu, in instituto persistit. In reliquis vero libris, saepe a se, simulque a Graecis degenerat, et retro cedit: qui vir curam et operam ubique ad Elegiam, nonnunquam gravitatem contulit. Reliqui longe ab hoc absunt, et Graecis hominibus res suas sibi habere iubent. Atqui liberrimum primo scribendi genus Elegia fuit: nos fortasse etiam audaculam fractamque fecimus. Eam postea coarctarunt cum alii, tum vel maxime ingeniosus Naso: qui quanvis, ingenii sui fraenos ubique laxet, ne frustra declamasse videatur; ut homo Romanus, artem constringit tamen, legemque, et aequabilitatem versuum sibi praescribit, cui ubique fere obtemperat. Sic cum tersissimo Tibulli filo animam addat, cultum non sustulit tamen. [...][100]

I have brought together in this *Monobiblos* in a kind of bundle compositions that are open, free, playful, unfettered, pleasant, and, in a word, Greek – the kind that tend to frighten Romans, on account of their joyfulness and rapidity of movement and ultimately their pleasure and charm. [...] Similarly that Catullus of ours, in some of his 'Greek' [verses], excelled as an affecter of unaffected elegance, as did Propertius, most of all in his first book, who, whenever he risks something beyond the Romans, calls himself Callimachus. But with the exception of one or two elegies, he did not give himself over to pleasure, and did not – whether because it was his firm intention or because his natural inclination swayed him otherwise – follow through on what he started. Instead in the rest of his books he deteriorates, often from himself as well as from the Greeks, and falls backwards. Propertius brought to elegy an effortful solicitude, and sometimes weightiness. The other [Roman elegists] are very far from this, and they file for divorce from the Greeks. And yet elegy was originally a very free genre: we too have, perhaps, made it a bit daring, and irregular. Later they and others fettered it, most of all the ingenious Ovid: who

---

100   Heinsius 1603: 123–4.

although he always gives free rein to his talent, so as to be seen to make the most of his declamations, still, being a Roman he constrains his art and the regulation of it, and he limits himself to uniform versification, with which he almost always complies. So although he breathes life into the extremely neat style of Tibullus, he did not take away its artificiality.

Heinsius's initial claim is somewhat surprising, since the *Monobiblos*, at least in terms of the models for its amatory content, is not really all that Greek.[101] In it Heinsius occasionally imitates Theocritus, and in the final poem (the farewell to his beloved, Rossa) he alludes to numerous Greek models and imagines an encounter with Anacreon and Pindar in the vale of Tempe; but that is a farewell to elegy and a promise to take up Greek authors and Greek themes in the future, a reaction to the exhortations of his teacher Joseph Scaliger.[102] Heinsius's most prominent models throughout the collection are still primarily the Roman elegists and Catullus – and Johannes Secundus.

What, then, explains his claim to have made Latin elegy Greek? van Dam is no doubt correct that Heinsius is evoking a general association of Greekness with eroticism and freedom, but I think there is something more specific in it than that. In saying that Ovid's version of elegy was too restrictive, and that Catullus and early Propertius were freer and thus closer to the Greeks, he is not talking primarily about the erotic content of the poetry: most readers would probably judge Ovid a 'freer' author than Propertius in this regard. His comments relate in particular to metrical form, as is clear from his criticism of the "uniform versification" of Ovid. The Ovidian elegiac couplet had been considered the exemplar of smoothness and fluency by earlier humanist grammarians and poets, in part because he almost always ended his pentameters with a disyllable and avoided polysyllabic endings, which were judged as a fault because they tended to inhibit the coincidence of word-accent and *ictus*. Heinsius, following Janus Dousa and others who had reacted against this prescription (on which see further below, pp. 99–101), is championing the more 'Greek' metrical practice of Catullus and early Propertius, which he associated with greater variation and freedom from artifice.

8   Women's Writing and Female Voices

Although there are several examples from the early modern period of women Latin poets, and many examples of women love poets, the intersection of these

---

101   van Dam 2008.
102   Orth 2008.

two sets is – as far as we know – a very slender one. Women who wrote and published Latin poetry did so in certain genres; their themes were predominantly
political and occasional, or religious.[103] There was a general view that learned
women should not compromise their reputation by attempting love poetry: the
stereotype of the 'learned maiden' – which dominated the bloated sub-genre
of male-authored epigrams in praise of women Latin poets – depended on
the equation of learning with chastity. Moreover, the dominant discourses of
Neo-Latin love poetry were highly gendered in ways that made them structurally resistant to the expression of female subjectivity and female desire.

Whereas love poetry in the classical mould – based, as it usually was, on the
idea of an extramarital love relationship – is exceedingly rare among women
Latin poets, there are a number of examples of love poetry celebrating married
love written in occasional genres such as the wedding-song and the funerary
lament. Some of these can be called 'love poetry' only in the loosest possible
sense. We can find female-authored *epithalamia*, but they do not have anything
of the personal feeling or frank eroticism of some of the male-authored works
of this type (see below, pp. 78–81): they are public poems composed for public
occasions. For example, an *epithalamium* composed by Henrietta Catharina
von Gersdorff (1648–1726) celebrates the marriage of Anna Sophie of Denmark
and Norway to Johann Georg III Elector of Saxony (1666).[104] The poem evokes
a certain sensualism in the opening descriptions of the Dawn and Venus, but
beyond this there is nothing that could be called love poetry – which would,
in any case, clearly be inappropriate in a poem whose point was to celebrate a
political alliance.

> Purpureas Matuta genas, ac plena rosarum
>   Ora, et odoratas exsere pulchra comas:
> Tuque fores aperi nascentis, et, alma, diei
>   Atria felici sidere pande, Venus.
> Aut si nostra sequi, Divae, consulta velitis,
>   Sub mare formarum condite grande decus.
> Pulchrius exoritur sidus, quod Baltica Thetys
>   Mittit in amplexus, SAXO VERENDE, Tuos.

> Beautiful Dawn, bring forth your blushing cheeks and your mouth full
> of roses and your scented tresses: and you, kind Venus, open the gates
> of the nascent day and grant entry under a fortunate star. Or if you wish

---

103   See the forthcoming Brill Research Perspectives volume on *Women and Latin in the Early
       Modern Period.*
104   Briefly discussed by Stevenson 2005: 339.

to follow our advice, goddesses, hide the great splendour of your beauty under the sea. A more beautiful star has risen, whom Baltic Thetys has sent into your embrace, noble Saxon.

On the other hand, we also see poems with a much more forceful emotional dimension in the genre of funerary elegy. Funerary lament was one of the genres most often practised by women Latin poets, and it offered greater scope for the expression of personal feeling. An example is Elizabeth Russell's (1540–1609) funerary poem for her first husband, Thomas Hoby, which reads very much like a love poem.

O dulcis conjux, animae pars maxima nostrae,
    Cujus erat vitae vita medulla meae,
Cur ita conjunctos divellunt invida fata?
    Cur ego sum viduo sola relicta thoro?
Anglia faelices, faelices Gallia vidit,
    Per mare, per terras noster abivit amor,
Par fortunatum fuimus dum viximus una,
    Corpus erat duplex, spiritus unus erat.
Sed nihil in terris durat charissime conjux
    Tu mihi, tu testis flebilis esse potes.

Beloved husband, greatest part of our soul,
whose life used to be the marrow of my life,
why are the malignant fates tearing apart people who were united in this
    way?
Why am I left alone in a widowed bed?
England saw us happy, France saw us happy,
our loves travelled away by sea and by land,
we were a fortunate pair so long as we lived together.
Our bodies were twofold: our spirit was one.
But, darling husband, nothing endures in this world,
you, O you, can be to me a witness fit to provoke tears.[105]

In women's writing throughout this period, the influence of classical and Petrarchan love lyric is far less evident in Latin poetry than it is in the vernacular. For example, Vittoria Colonna (1492–1547) and Veronica Gambara (1485–1550) were both prolific love poets and accomplished Latinists, but

---

105   Trans. by J. Stevenson (Stevenson 2005: 267–8).

their love poems were in Italian, and the few Latin poems they wrote were non-erotic.[106] Perhaps the most famous woman love poet of the Renaissance, Louise Labé (*c.*1522–1566) – who did not write Latin poetry but almost certainly did know Latin – clearly read the love elegists and Ovid's *Heroides*, and imitated them in her French elegies and sonnets.[107]

Another Italian Latinist, Tarquinia Molza (1542–1617) was renowned for her work on Greek philosophy, and in particular for her interest in Platonic theories of love.[108] She was a poet and musician, but again her Latin poems are not amatory in theme. The following commendatory epigram, in its opening lines, co-opts Molza into the genre of love elegy, but casts her as the *docta puella* rather than as the elegiac poet: the object and not the subject of the amatory discourse:

> In lucem redeat si qui tibi Lesbia nomen,
>   Cynthia quique dedit, Delia quique tibi,
> Tarquiniae formam non sat per carmina fingam,
>   Nec Cous Pictor exprimat in tabulis.[109]

If the one who granted you your renown, Lesbia, were to come back to life, or the one who granted yours, Cynthia, or yours, Delia, I could not sufficiently express the beauty of Tarquinia in poetry, nor could the artist of Kos [Apelles] represent it in painting.

This anonymous poem makes the move (very typical in works of this type) of reducing Tarquinia to her physical beauty (her "forma"), bypassing completely her accomplishments as a poet, musician and scholar: it is this quality for which she merits comparison to the *puellae* of the elegists, who owe their renown, their very names, to the male poets who granted them. We see something similar happening with Cassandra Fedele (*c.*1465–1558), one of the most brilliant women scholars of the Italian Renaissance, reduced to comparison with the 'learned' Corinna of Ovid and Cynthia of Propertius.[110] In comparing

---

106 On the Petrarchan love poetry of Gambara and Colonna see Cox 2005 and (more generally) 2008: 64–75. On Gambara's and Colonna's Latin poetry, Stevenson 2005: 169–171, 447, 469–470.

107 Sterritt 2005.

108 Stevenson 2005: 290. Tarquinia Molza was also cast as the speaker in two different dialogues on love by Torquato Tasso and Francesco Patrizi (Cox 2008: 138).

109 Molza 1750: 28.

110 "Peligni doctam sileat modo carta Corinnam / Cedat et Aurelii Cynthia culta modis." (Let the page now keep silent about the learned Corinna of Ovid and let Cynthia cultivated by

these women Latin poets to the *doctae puellae* of Roman love elegy, the authors of these epigrams are picking up on the elements of the elegiac discourse that grant women a mind and voice of their own, but always heavily circumscribed and contained by the male-authored poetic discourse. The comparison to the *docta puella* or *culta puella* is thus little different from the discourse that would compare women to fictional exemplary women of myth and legend.

The epigram is, though, more interesting than it seems: after likening Molza to Lesbia, Cynthia and Delia, its author contrives to refocus the comparison on Catullus, Propertius and Tibullus themselves. Indeed, Molza outdoes those poets, since only she is capable of expressing in poetry the superlative nature of her own beauty: "May she alone portray herself, nor think it shameful to her, since she is the only one capable of representing her own beauty" ("se sola effingat, sibi nec putet esse pudori, / cum proprium possit sola referre decus"). Molza is both the object and the subject of the discourse of love poetry: the poem becomes entangled in its own premise. Its author lacks a way of talking about female poetic talent other than as an exception and a paradox.

There were, of course, ancient models for first-person love poetry by women writers: Sappho and Sulpicia. The name of Sappho was a constant reference point in laudatory pieces on women poets, but the Sappho they praised was usually no more than a name, the proverbial 'tenth Muse'.[111] For most readers of the fifteenth and sixteenth centuries, the version of Sappho most familiar to them was the Sappho ventriloquized by Ovid in the *Heroides*. The *Epistula Sapphus* was taken to be a genuine work of Sappho by some of the early humanists: Beccadelli in 1426 wrote that the verses of Sappho of Lesbos "survive in a Latin version", which he found "so immodest, so provocative, and yet so elegant that they stir the loins of anybody who reads them".[112] Beccadelli approved, but for most the Sappho of Latin elegy was a target of opprobrium and misogynistic satire, largely held at arm's length from the praiseworthy Sappho. The real Sappho awaited the editorial efforts of Henri Estienne (in 1560/66), and later Anne Dacier (1647–1720), who issued a commented translation into French of the fragments in 1681; although her genuine works were imitated by women poets, there is (so far) little to say about her reception in Latin love lyric by women.

If some readers mistook Ovid's false Sappho for the real one, the inverse is true of Sulpicia: the elegiacs which are considered by many today to be by a

---

the strains of Propertius give way). This MS epigram "Ad Cassandram Fidelem poetissam" can be found at <http://www.poetiditalia.it/texts/FEDELE|epig|oo1>.

111   Overviews of Sappho's early modern reception: Gillespie 2021; Piantanida 2021.
112   Beccadelli 2010: 116–117.

real woman poet were for most of the period taken to be the work of Tibullus. Nobody (with some notable exceptions: Barth, Brouckhusius) seems to have taken them seriously as works of a woman poet until the nineteenth century.[113]

Primarily for this reason, Sulpicia is not generally thought to have been taken up as a model by early modern women poets, and there is little scholarship on this aspect of Sulpicia's reception.[114] There is, however, at least one example of female-authored Latin love elegy from much later in the period, which is written partly in imitation of Sulpicia. Caterina Borghini, known as 'Erato Dionea', a member of the Accademia degli Arcadi, was the author of two Latin elegies, "Oculi nigri" and "Oculi caerulei" (c.1730 and first published in print in 1826).[115] The titular theme suggests Petrarchism, but the language and style of the poems are strongly influenced by the classical elegists, and we can find precedents in Neo-Latin love poetry of cycles of poems devoted to the mistress's eyes, such as Janus Lernutius's *Ocelli* (1614). Borghini was said by Francesco Pentolini to have written in the style of Tibullus,[116] a claim now repeated whenever she is mentioned; however, on the evidence of these elegies, I would suggest that it was more specifically the Sulpicia poems ([Tibullus] 3.8–18) that served as Borghini's model.

> Praecipue his oculis (nam deperit omnia pulcra)
>   Haeret inexpleto lumine fixus Amor;
> Cumque supercilii, nigrique colore capilli
>   Suspicit ille rosas, suspicit ille nives.
> Luminibus captum quis fingere primus Amorem
>   Ausus? Plus oculis omnibus ille videt.
> Et videt, et sine fine nigros intentus ocellos,
>   Phylli, videns, visu non satiatur Amor.
> Ut sibi formosa gavisus imagine plaudit!
>   Ut pulcram toto pectore pulcher amat!
> Heu quae bella deis, quae praelia dura minatur,
>   Hos si oculos castos possit habere duces!
> At cupidi illecebras artesque repellit Amoris,
>   Seque deo facilem Phyllis amata negat.
>   "Oculi nigri" 29–42

---

113   Skoie 2002: 9.

114   An exception is Grant 2019: 151–188, who seeks general parallels between Sulpicia and some sixteenth-century English women writers, but finds no evidence of direct influence.

115   A modern edition based on the 1826 publication can be found in Borghini 2001. There are two other elegies by Borghini in *Arcadum Carmina* 1756: 96–100.

116   Pentolini 1776: 233.

Amor especially (for he dies with love for all that is beautiful) clings to those eyes, fixed by their inexhaustible gaze. And together with the colour of her brow, and her black hair, he admires the roses, and admires the snows [of her complexion]. Who first dared to imagine Amor blinded in the eyes? He sees more than all eyes. He sees, and seeing your black eyes, endlessly straining towards them, Phyllis, Amor is never sated by seeing. How he congratulates himself, rejoicing in this beautiful vision! How he in his beauty loves her in her beauty with all his heart! Alas, what wars, what harsh battles are threatened for the gods, if he can have those chaste eyes as his leaders! But Phyllis repels the charms and arts of lustful Amor, and, though loved by a god, refuses to yield herself to him.

This poem contains numerous echoes of [Tib.] 3.8, that is, the first poem of the so-called "Garland of Sulpicia". Borghini writes: "Denique quidquid agit, vel quo vestigia virgo, / Quo fert cumque gradus, imminet acer Amor" (In the end whatever she does, wherever the maid turns her steps, harsh Amor bears down on her, 55–6), alluding to the description of Sulpicia: "Illam, quidquid agit, quoquo vestigia movit, / componit furtim subsequiturque Decor" (8.7–8). Borghini's line "Vellera in oebalio bis madefacta cado" (wool twice soaked in a Spartan jar, 50) echoes the verse of the Sulpicia poem "vellera det sucis bis madefacta Tyros" (8.16).

The poem that Borghini imitates here is one of those attributed to the *amicus Sulpiciae*, that is to say a poem about her rather than by her (although arguments have been advanced in favour of reading the whole sequence 8–18 as authored by Sulpicia). In the sequence Sulpicia takes on different roles in the elegiac discourse: she is both object of the erotic gaze (in the third person poems 3.8, 3.10, 3.12) and writing, desiring subject (in the first person poems 3.9, 3.11, 3.13–18).[117] Borghini's "Oculi" elegies, partly through their engagement with Sulpicia, thus revel in the entanglements of subject and object that we observed in the epigram to Molza. In them, Borghini assumes the masculine elegiac perspective directing the poetic gaze at the female object of desire. But Amor, as he gazes at the eyes of Phyllis, becomes a Narcissus figure (Borghini makes repeated allusions to Ovid's Narcissus narrative), seeing himself in the mirror of her eyes and, never sated by seeing, is defeated and must learn to look with chaste passion. Her eyes win their victory in the closing lines of the poem:

---

117   On this aspect see Skoie 2012.

At vos, discussa somni caligine, ocelli,
  Aetherias vigili vincite luce faces.
Vincite: dumque videt vos, ardescitque videndo
  Ignibus innocuis fervere discat Amor.
      "Oculi nigri" 75–8

But you, eyes, shake off the fog of sleep and overcome the lights of heaven with your wakeful gaze. Overcome: and may Amor, seeing you, and inflamed by seeing, learn how to burn with desires that harm not.

Borghini's complex game of mirroring and inversion of the subject and object of writing, seeing and desiring, and its implications for the construction of gender in female authored elegy, deserve fuller critical attention.

In Latin, love poetry from a female first-person perspective was more often written by men ventriloquizing the female voice than by women poets. We find non-epistolary forms of love poetry written in the person of women, connected with the rhetorical exercise of *ethopoeia* (impersonation), such as the elegiac monologue of Andromeda by Janus Pannonius (1434–1472).[118] But the dominant form was the verse epistle after the model of Ovid's *Heroides*. The *Heroides*, a collection of fictive letters in elegiacs from mythological or historical women to the men who have abandoned them (with some replies in the so-called 'double *Heroides*', 16–21), had an important reception in the Renaissance and was much imitated in Neo-Latin poetry.[119] The keynote of the letters in Ovid's collection is lament and vituperation, but they also adopt the idioms and conventions of love elegy, and were taken up by Renaissance poets as models of amatory complaint and persuasion.

The most tenacious Neo-Latin imitator of the *Heroides* was the Scottish poet Mark Alexander Boyd (1562–1601), who wrote not one but two full books of *Heroides*.[120] The first compiles his compositions written from the perspective of the male respondents to Ovid's heroines, but the second (*Epistulae Heroides*, 1592) consists of love letters written in the person of women from myth and Roman history, including one from the love goddess herself to her beloved Adonis on his death. It is notable in particular for the way in which Boyd goes

---

118   Jankovits 2014.
119   Dörrie 1968 remains the essential reference point.
120   The second of these has a modern edition: Boyd 2010. The earlier collection is discussed in White 2009: 207–243.

against the grain of Renaissance attitudes towards the sexual morality of Ovid's heroines to present a more positive view of female sexual freedom.[121]

Although Neo-Latin epistolary elegies in direct imitation of the *Heroides* continued to be written throughout the period (including poems in the person of contemporary women), there were comparatively few complete books of poems in the genre. There were, though, numerous collections in the sub-genre of *Heroides sacrae*: Christian versions of Ovid's epistles that substituted Biblical figures and saints for the mythological heroines, and transposed the discourse of erotic love, persuasion and lament to the language of Christian devotion, proselytism and martyrdom. The first and best known of these collections was the *Heroidum Christianarum epistolae* (1514) by the German poet Helius Eobanus Hessus (1488–1540). These "Letters of Christian Heroines" (which Hessus reissued in a new form in 1532 in response to Lutheran antipathy to the use of non-Scriptural sources) slip in and out of the amatory language used by Ovid's heroines; its terms are overlaid with Christian meanings, the earthly desires of the elegiac heroines converted to spiritual yearnings. Hessus's *Heroides sacrae* have received some scholarly attention in recent years, aided by the appearance of Vredeveld's edition of his poetic works.[122] A less studied, but no less interesting, work by a Catholic poet is the *Sacrarum Heroidum liber* (1564) of Claude d'Espence (1511–1571). It consists of elegiac epistles written in the person of women expressing their love and devotion for Apostles or rebutting the amorous advances of pagan rulers, with subjects taken from Acts (Tabitha or Dorcas), from the Apocrypha (Drusiana; Thecla), from the hagiographical literature (Iphigenia) and from the Old Testament (Susanna). The elegiac currency of sighs and tears, of expressions of passionate devotion and amatory persuasion, is converted to Christian tender. The metaphor d'Espence prefers for this process of conversion is that of the purification of a captive woman for marriage by shaving and paring the "dead parts of her body" (hair and fingernails), an image used by Saint Jerome to justify the use of pagan sources in Christian writing.[123] In d'Espence's use, the figure of the captive woman implies an identification of the text with the bodies of the writing heroines. D'Espence intends his rewriting of Ovid's *Heroides* to de-sexualize the Ovidian heroine, to get her dangerous passions under control, and to pare

121   Paleit 2008.
122   Hessus 2008. Some attention has also been given to later works in the same vein by Jesuit poets such as Jacob Bidermann (1578–1639), Balduinus Cabillavius (1568–1652), Jean Vincart (1593–1679) and Jacob Balde (1604–1668), in which the amatory dimension is less prominent and the cast of letter writers is expanded to include men: see Eickmeyer 2014.
123   D'Espence 1564: 7–9. The Jerome text is *Ep.* LXX; the account of the captive women refers to Deut. 21:10–14. Erasmus also used this example in the first version of the *Antibarbari*.

her excessive language down to the Christian essentials. To write as a woman, to present a model of how a woman should write of love, is to discipline the captive female body.

D'Espence's close literary and spiritual association with the Dominican nun and poet Anne de Marquets (*c*.1533–1588) suggests a further line for research in this area to pursue: links between Neo-Latin love poetry and female-authored devotional poetry in the vernacular. Anne de Marquets translated many of d'Espence's Latin verses into French, and although she appears not to have taken up d'Espence's *Heroides sacrae* as a model, she did also translate Marcantonio Flaminio's *Carminum sacrorum libellus* (as *Les Divines Poesies de Marc Antoine Flaminius* (1568–1569)). These translations, and her original sonnets, merge Christian devotional themes with the language and *topoi* of classical and Petrarchan love poetry.[124]

9   Philosophical and Spiritual Currents

9.1   *Biblical Themes*

During the Reformation, love poetry was forced into the fray of theological polemic, and often emerged a casualty. As we have seen with the *querelle* over the *Poemata* of Théodore de Bèze, individual works of classicizing erotic poetry might simply be a pretext for, or collateral damage in, otherwise unrelated disputes. Such was the argument Bèze himself wanted to make, although it is noteworthy that even while striving to downplay the relevance of his erotic poetry to his theology, he himself used it to mock the theology of his opponents. In answering the accusation that the 'Publia' of one of his love poems was a real person, he wrote:

> Poeticos meos lusus quum ut res serio dictas et scriptas interpretaris, quis te iudex aequus audiat? Ubi quaeso Publia illa viri quem adhuc superstitem dicis uxor? Hoc enim coram Deo iuratus testari possum, non magis unquam mihi contigisse ut cuiusquam uxoris pudicitiam attentarem, quam ut Indorum regnum invaderem. Testor et illud, tam fictitiam esse Publiam illam cuius forte in Elegia quadam memini, quam est vester panaceus Deus, quo ne chimaeram quidem inaniorem esse prorsus credo.[125]

---

124   Macaskill 2015.
125   "Ad F. Claudii de Xainctes responsionem altera Th. Bezae apologia" (Bèze 1573: 400).

When you interpret my poetic games as things said and written in seriousness, what judge would give you a fair hearing? Where, pray, is that
'Publia' – wife to a man who (you say) is still alive? I can testify and swear
before God that it has never occurred to me to defile the virtue of anyone's wife, any more than it has to invade India. I swear this too, that the
Publia I once happened to mention in one of my elegies is just as fictional
as your breadish God: not even the Chimera (I absolutely believe) has less
substance than that!

Bèze's argument here appears to be a rather superficial one – his opponent is
just as confused about poetic fictions as he is about points of theology – but
it does have a point in connection with the poem itself. The poem to which
he refers here (*Elegiae* 3) is one that plays on the Ovidian elegiac theme of
absence and presence, and does so, we might say, in a typically Ovidian metal-
iterary way: Publia's absence in the poem is of a piece with her fictionality.
(The question 'Where is Publia?' is posed in the poem itself, as well as here.)
The Catholic adversary's failure of imagination in misunderstanding the ludic
dimension of literature is connected with his doctrinal failure in asserting the
real presence of Christ in the Eucharist.

There was also, for Bèze, a deeper and more serious connection between
love poetry and his religious ideas. Other poems printed in the 1548 *Iuvenilia*
(which he did not later disown) also made use of the language and images of
classical love poetry to treat religious themes. His *Silva* 4, a hexameter poem
narrating the story of David's adulterous love for Bathsheba and his killing of
her husband Uriah (2 Samuel 11–12), is an exploration of concepts of sin, sal-
vation, and grace couched in the idioms of classical love poetry and epic. The
text, in which the pagan love god Cupid plays a key role, develops in a complex
allusive relationship with the *Aeneid* of Virgil and the *Amores* of Ovid.[126]

This example reminds us that the Bible provided Neo-Latin poets of all
confessions with abundant subject matter for love poems, and indeed con-
tained its own examples of love poetry. Filippo Beroaldo (1453–1505) in his
Oratio in Propertium had pointed out that those who wish to reject texts deal-
ing with amatory themes must also throw out the Old Testament books of
Genesis, Numbers, Judges, Esther, Kings, and of course the Song of Solomon.
The Song of Solomon was a favourite reference point for the early Renaissance
Neo-Platonic philosophers who wished to align Plato's philosophy of love with
Biblical sources. And numerous Neo-Latin love poets would draw on it for their

---

126   Nassichuk 2008.

own compositions. One of the most famous and influential was the Polish Jesuit poet Maciej Kazimierz Sarbiewski (1595–1640). Sarbiewski's lyric paraphrases of the Song of Solomon express their religious subjects in Horatian metres and with the language of classical and Petrarchan love poetry.[127] "surround me with rose petals, with the crocus and the violet", he writes, "for waiting for my Lord whom I have seen has inflamed my soul in holy fire".[128] "You kept saying as you departed 'Farewell my bride'; and your flowing steps instantly surpassed the clouds, and you have brought great longing to my heart, Jesus".[129] These are love poems to Christ, as is the "Dialogus Pueri Jesu et Virginis Matris", a Marian devotional poem based on the Song of Solomon which reads as a "filigreed love-duet sung antiphonally by the Babe and His Mother".[130]

Puer: Sic fulges oculis, ut geminus prope,
Qui cum lusit agris fons Eseboniis,
Clausum stare quieto
Se miratur in otio.

Virgo: Sic luces oculis, ut geminae prope
Lucent, seu fluvio, sive liquentibus
Lotae lacte columbae
Assedere canalibus.

Child: Your sparkling eyes two Silver streams surpass,
    That near to *Essebon* do stray,
Which when they long have bubl'd o're the grass,
    And sported long in wanton play,
Wonder to find their wand'ring Streams supprest,
To bounds confin'd, and husht in calms of rest.

Virgin: Your shining Eyes as clear, and spotless look
    As two white Doves in Milk washt o're,
Which sit upon the Bank of some fair Brook,
    Or some transparent Rivers shore:

---

127 See in particular those collected in the anthology of Mertz (ed.) 1989: 20–3; 36–7.
128 "Me stipate rosariis: / Me fulcite crocis: me violariis [...] nam visi mora Numinis / Mi sacris animam torret in ignibus" (2.25).
129 "Dicebas abiens: Sponsa vale; simul / Vicisti liquidis nubila passibus. / Longam ducis, Iesu, / In desideriis moram" (4.29).
130 Kraszewski 2006: 36.

Yet from those Balls of Snow bright flashes fly,
More swift then Lightning darted from the Sky.[131]

In the seventeenth century, Jesuit poets also continued to take up the model of Latin love elegy, reconfiguring its erotic discourse to offer up a Christian corrective to the vision of profane love it presented: "Discite quid sit Amor" ("Learn what Love is"), admonished Sidronius Hosschius (1596–1653) in an elegy on Christ's passion.[132] Although it would not be stretching the definition of 'love poetry' beyond its breaking point to admit here many other examples of Christian devotional poetry in Latin, and to explore the interanimation in poetry of sacred and profane love, to do so would be to expand the compass of this study to monstrous proportions.

9.2   Neo-Platonism

Leonardo Bruni, to whom the first Neo-Latin love elegist Giovanni Marrasio dedicated his *Angelinetum*,[133] wrote that Marrasio's elegies ranked him with Propertius, Tibullus and Ovid; but he insisted in a famous letter to Marrasio that they should be interpreted in quite different terms from those of elegiac love:

> Poetarum ergo furor a Musis est; amantium vero a Venere. Oritur autem hic ex verae pulchritudinis contemplatione, cuius effigiem visu intuentes acerrimo ac violentissimo sensuum nostrorum, stupentes ac velut extra nos positi, totis affectibus in illum corripimur, ut non minus vere quam eleganter dictum sit amantis animam in alieno corpore vitam ducere. Haec igitur vehemens occupatio animi atque correptio amor vocatur: divina quaedam alienatio ac veluti sui ipsius oblivio et in id quoius pulchritudinem admiramur transfusio. Quam si furorem ac vesaniam appellas, concedam etiam atque fatebor, dummodo intelligas neque poetam bonum esse ullum posse nisi huiusmodi furore correptum, neque futura praevidere vaticinantes, nisi per huiusmodi furorem, neque perfecte neque eximie deum coli, nisi per huiusmodi mentis alienationem.

Thus, while the poet's madness derives from the Muses, that of lovers comes from Venus. It arises moreover from the beholding of true beauty;

---

131   *Lyricorum libri IV*, 4.25.9–16. The translation comes from *Miscellany Poems and Translations by Oxford Hands* (Oxford: Anthony Stephens, 1685) and is quoted in Kraszweski 2006: 36. See also Forster 1978: 8–9 for analysis of the Petrarchan elements of this poem.
132   On Hosschius's devotional elegies (*Elegiarum libri sex*, 1656), see Houghton 2017: 109–111.
133   Above, p. 7.

looking at its image with the most passionate and violent gaze, con-
founded and, as it were, placed outside ourselves, we are carried away
with all the feelings of our senses fastened on it, so that it might be said
no less truly than elegantly that the soul of the lover lives in another's
body. Therefore this violent possession and seizure of the mind is called
love: it is a certain divine alienation and, as it were, forgetfulness of self
and a transformation into that thing whose beauty we marvel at. If you
call this madness and insanity, I shall even grant it and admit it as long
as you understand that no poet can be good unless seized by such madness, nor can anyone who makes predictions foresee the future unless by
madness of this sort, nor can god be worshipped perfectly and excellently
unless by that same alienation of mind.[134]

This is an early formulation of the philosophy of love that would eventually
be elaborated into what we now call Renaissance Neo-Platonism. When modern critics speak casually of the presence of 'Neo-Platonism' in early modern
love poetry, what is normally meant is not the vast and complex thought-world
of ancient Neo-Platonism (Plotinus, Porphyry, Iamblichus), but a set of
ideas, images and themes that largely derived from one specific work: the
De amore of Marsilio Ficino (1433–1499). Ficino's work (which itself drew on
ancient Neo-Platonism, particularly Plotinus), packaged Platonic love into a
Christianizing and morally unthreatening version that appealed to humanist
love poets. Ficino was not the only *Quattrocento* humanist to work on the reha-
bilitation of Platonic love: Bruni, Bessarion and Pico della Mirandola were his
predecessors, and other Florentine thinkers made important contributions,
among them Cristoforo Landino. But Ficino's work – and especially his *De
amore*, a commentary on the *Symposium* (1469; first printed 1484) – was by far
the most influential. That work aligned Plato's philosophy of love as expressed
in the *Symposium* to a Christian framework, insisting that the same-sex love
promoted by Plato was chaste, and emphasizing "its place within an elaborate
system of Neo-Platonic metaphysics".[135]

  The main components of the philosophy of love set out by Ficino in the
De amore were as follows.[136] According to the doctrine of the 'two Venuses',
there are two types of love: corporeal and spiritual. The former is praiseworthy
insofar as it leads to procreation, but the latter, which is intellectual and the

---

134 Trans. by Mary P. Chatfield. Marrasio 2016: 46–7.
135 Kraye 1994: 78.
136 Concise accounts are to be found in Kraye 1994, Panizza 2011, and in the edition of Pierre
     Laurens (Ficino 2002).

true 'Platonic love', is to be preferred. The 'divine alienation' experienced in the contemplation of physical beauty (described by Bruni in the quotation above) might lead the lover's soul to ascend Diotima's ladder from the corporeal to the divine realm of the One, understood as the Christian God. The means by which God draws the soul from the lower world back to the higher is the divine madness or frenzy, which manifests in four types (described in Plato's *Phaedrus*), of which the frenzies belonging to love and to poetry are the most important, according to Ficino in the *De divino furore* (1457). The linking of the frenzy of poetic inspiration (*furor poeticus*) with the frenzy of love (*furor amatorius*) would become a key idea in Neo-Latin love poetry.

The influence of philosophy on Neo-Latin love poetry was important, but perhaps equally so was the role of love poetry in furnishing material for philosophy and in shaping its language and concepts. Clearly Ficino's philosophical conception of love was formed in large part by his reading of Petrarchan and classical love poetry, and by his discussions with contemporary love poets. Naldo Naldi (1439–1513), who would be a member of the Florentine Academy and close friend of Marsilio Ficino, wrote a collection of love elegies – completed in the early 1470s but begun in his early youth. His *Eleg.* 1.4, dedicated to Ficino, sets out to explain the symptoms of love to his friend:

> Quid mirare, meo cur sit modo pallor in ore,
> > Cur faciem macies occupet usque meam?
> Nescis, heu, nescis, ut me meus urgeat error
> > Cupidineus vexet, amice, furor.
> Nam si parva tibi veniat scintilla caloris,
> > Qui mihi perpetua conterit ossa face,
> Cur fruar, heu, potius, certe miraberis, aura
> > Curve queam tantis sic superesse malis

How is it that you wonder why there is now pallor in my face, and why gauntness constantly affects my looks? You know not, ah! you know not how my folly oppresses me, and how the frenzy of desire plagues me. For if there came to you a tiny spark of the heat that wastes my bones with unceasing fire, you would surely instead wonder why I derive pleasure from the air, or why I am able to survive such great ills.

Della Torre reckoned that this poem was written by Naldi to Ficino shortly after 1451, when Ficino was 18 years old and not yet familiar with love.[137] Here we see

---

137   Della Torre 1902: 506.

how the language that Ficino would later use to explain the effects of love in physiological and metaphysical terms was being used in the poetic discourse on love ("Cupidineus furor"; "scintilla caloris"; and for the elegiac "pallor" and "macies" (cf. *Symposium* 203c–e) compare the physiological explanation at *De amore* 6.9).

Filippo Beroaldo the Elder's *Oratio in Propertium de amore* (first printed 1491), which set elegiac love squarely in the interpretative framework of Platonism, became an important document for the dissemination of Neo-Platonic ideas in France and northern Europe, thanks largely to the assiduous promotional efforts of Jodocus Badius Ascensius. Beroaldo begins by saying that he will follow the example of Socrates in his second speech in the *Phaedrus*, and will set out to praise love freely and without shame, since love, and love poetry, are worthy of the highest praise. The role of the love elegists in Beroaldo's conception is a priestly one, not diminished by the apparent triviality and worldliness of elegiac love.

> Ceterum cum ille qui deum colit amet et sacerdotes: Nos qui amoris cultores esse volumus. diligamus illius sacerdotes. qui profecto sunt poetae amasii atque elegiographi: quorum lepidiora poemata non sunt spernanda neque pro argumento impudiciciae sunt habenda: et quamvis vetus verbum sit talem esse hominum vitam qualis sit oratio tamen poetis ludere versiculis amatoriis et lascivire permittitur.[138]

> Moreover, since those who worship God love his priests too, we who wish to be devotees of love should esteem its priests, who are surely the love poets and the elegists; their charming poems should not be rejected or taken as evidence of shamelessness, and although the ancient saying is that a person's life matches his speech, still it is permitted to poets to play with light verses about love and to indulge in licence.

Beroaldo further developed these ideas in the dedicatory letter of his *Commentarii in Propertium* (1487). There, he wrote of the divine inspiration of love poets, and, quoting from Plato's *Ion*, described the poetic frenzy of inspiration which radiates magnetically to affect also its rhapsodes or interpreters. The ideal reader of his commentary (identified with his dedicatee, Mino Roscio) would be one "who has himself served in the squadron of Venus, who has been a follower of Love; I mean of that Love that is the most blessed, the most

---

138   Beroaldo 1491: a.vi^r.

beautiful, the best, that makes us friends of the gods, which Plato in the *Symposium* shows to be heavenly and precious."[139]

One persistent motif of Neo-Latin love poetry that is usually identified by critics as a Neo-Platonic feature is the idea of the transfer of souls via a kiss. Ficino had written that love is a kind of willing death ("mors voluntaria"), and in situations of reciprocal love the soul of the lover leaves his body to live on in the body of the other, and *vice versa* ("quotiens duo aliqui mutua se benevolentia complectuntur, iste in illo, ille in isto vivit").[140] But the 'Platonic kiss' itself is not actually in Plato or indeed in Ficino. It stems ultimately from a pseudo-Platonic epigram (cited, for example, by Beroaldo in his *Oratio in Propertium*), which Renaissance writers found it easy to absorb into Ficino's formulation of the metaphysics of love – "When I kiss Agathon my soul is on my lips, where it comes, poor thing, hoping to cross over" – and from the extended version of in in Latin iambic dimeters included in Aulus Gellius *Noctes Atticae* 19.11.[141]

Two frequently cited examples will illustrate the ways Neo-Latin love poets varied the pseudo-Platonic theme, combining it with classical and Petrarchan motifs and elaborating it with evocations of Platonic/Ficinian ideas about love, but essentially aiming less at philosophical consistency or coherency than at enjoyment of its convolutions and ironies. First, Marullus:

> Suaviolum invitae rapio dum, casta Neaera,
> Imprudens vestris liqui animam in labiis,
> Exanimusque diu, cum nec per se ipsa rediret
> Et mora letalis quantulacumque foret,
> Misi cor quaesitum animam; sed cor quoque blandis
> Captum oculis nunquam deinde mihi rediit.
> Quod nisi suaviolo flammam quoque, casta Neaera,
> Hausissem, quae me sustinet exanimum,
> Ille dies misero, mihi crede, supremus amanti
> Luxisset, rapui cum tibi suaviolum.
> *Epig.* 2.4.1–6

---

139 "qui stipendia fecit in Veneris contubernio, qui fuit assecla cupidinis; illius, inquam, cupidinis qui beatissimus, pulcherrimus, optimus est; qui nos diis amicos facit; quem Plato in Symposio celestem pretiosumque esse autumat" (Beroaldo 1487: a.iii[r]).
140 *De amore* 2.8 (Ficino 2002: 43–5).
141 Ludwig 1989b; Wong 2017: 136–200. Wong notes (142–3) that an influential Neo-Platonic exposition of the soul-kiss is found in Castiglione, *Libro del Cortegiano* 4 (1528).

As I was snatching a kiss from you against your will, O chaste Neaera, unwittingly I left my soul upon your lips and I remained unconscious for a long time. When it did not return on its own and even the slightest delay might prove fatal, I sent my heart in search of my soul; but my heart too, captured by your sweet glances, has never returned to me since. If I had not also absorbed with that kiss the flame that sustains my lifeless body, chaste Neaera, that day, believe me, when I snatched that kiss from you, would have been the last to shine upon this hapless lover.[142]

The epigram is a combination of the pseudo-Platonic concept of the exchange of souls in a kiss with imitation of Catullus 99 (the stolen kiss), seasoned with Petrarchan conceits. The idea of the lover's death, which is not present in the Platonic epigram but which is there as a suggestion in the Latin version quoted by Gellius, is indebted to Ficino, who in *De amore* 2.8 describes the death of the lover in situations of unreciprocated love.[143]

Marullus writes to a "chaste" and unyielding mistress; Johannes Secundus addresses his mistress – also 'Neaera' – in a state of post-coital exhaustion ("languidus e dulci certamine"). The conceit of this poem (*Basium* 13) is that the persona is on the point of death when his lover Neaera's kiss revives his body by transferring part of her soul to him, even as he watches his own soul pass over to the beyond. It concludes:

Pars animae, mea Vita, tuae hoc in corpore vivit,
    et dilapsuros sustinet articulos;
quae tamen impatiens in pristina iura reverti
    saepe per arcanas nititur aegra vias.
Ac, nisi dilecta per te foveatur ab aura,
    iam collabentes deserit articulos.
Ergo age, labra meis innecte tenacia labris,
    assidueque duos spiritus unus alat;
donec, inexpleti post taedia sera furoris,
    unica de gemino corpore vita fluet.

Part of your soul, o my life, is living in this body of mine, and is sustaining my failing limbs; but it is restless and strains weakly to return to its former seat of power by secret routes. And unless it is nourished by your

---

142   Marullus 2012: 54–5. Translation by Charles Fantazzi. See the discussions of this poem in
      Ludwig 1989b: 440–1, Ford 2013: 62–3 and Wong 2017: 149–50.
143   Ford 2013: 63 n.13.

dear breath, it will desert my limbs which are already collapsing. So act now, join your lips fast to my lips, and let one continual breath support two, until, long weary of unsatisfied passion, a single life will flow from a double body.

The image in the final couplet glances at the Androgyne myth of the *Symposium* (a reference that is brought out more fully by Marc-Antoine Muret when he closely imitates this couplet in his *Elegiae*).[144] The version of Neo-Platonic doctrine presented in Secundus's poem is rather garbled, but philosophical coherency is not its point. It is of a piece with the tonal inconsistency of the poem, which could be read as an ironic and subversive treatment of the Neo-Platonic theme – the sexual meanings tending to undermine the seriousness of the vision of spiritual union[145] – but might equally be viewed as a finely wrought and delicately balanced expression of contradictory impulses.[146]

9.3   *Lucretius*

The same literary culture in Naples that had first given impetus to Neo-Catullanism was also important for the poetic reception of Lucretius: Pontano, Marullus and Sannazaro all wrote poetry in imitation of Lucretius's Epicurean philosophical epic *De rerum natura*. The opening of Lucretius's poem, the so-called "Hymn to Venus", was frequently imitated in both vernacular and Latin poetry. One of its first Neo-Latin imitators was also one of the first editors of the text of Lucretius, Michael Marullus. Marullus's *Hymni naturales* include hymns to Amor (1.3) and to Venus (2.7), both in Sapphic stanzas, both drawing on the Lucretian model and Neo-Platonic philosophy to present love as the cosmic force that governs the universe.[147] Those poems present a rather impersonal conception of love; in Lucretius's own philosophical vision, erotic desire and indeed sex played a far more fundamental role, and not only in the parts of book 4 of the *De rerum natura* where the subject is sex. As a consequence of the explosion of interest in recent years in the early modern reception of Lucretius,[148] the importance of Lucretian reception in love lyric is now beginning to receive attention; one recent study of the erotic dimension of Lucretius

144   "Quin tandem ambiguae post iura precaria lucis / Unicus e gemino spiritus ore fluat." See the discussion by Leroux 2015: 68–70.
145   For a reading of this poem on these lines, see Wong 2017: 176–9.
146   Paul Desforges-Maillard, for example, wrote in a letter to Voltaire that "cette petite pièce vaut, selon moi, tout ce qu'Anacréon et Tibulle ont fait de plus délicat".
147   See the commentary of Chomarat in Marullus 1995: 44–51, 128–139. Also Rees 2018.
148   Among many others see in particular Palmer 2014 and Hardie et al. 2016.

reception in early modern vernacular poetry indicates a line that could fruit-fully be pursued further in relation to Neo-Latin love poetry.[149]

Lucretius's account of the futility of erotic desire – according to which the lover strives in vain to possess the substance of the desired object, hav-ing been stimulated by its *simulacrum*, the insubstantial film of atoms that conveys the image of it to the senses[150] – has been shown to underpin the language and themes of Roman love elegy and of Ovid's Narcissus narrative in the *Metamorphoses*.[151] Lucretian *simulacra* and delusive images permeate Neo-Latin love poetry, sometimes through the filter of Ovid's Narcissus, or via the visions and dreams that plague and deceive the elegiac lover. Lucretian language also haunts contexts far removed from his materialist explanation of human delusions: the Petrarchan untouchable object of desire and the Ficinian conception of the image of the beloved prompting ascent to the divine. Paulus Melissus, for example, presents in the following lines a description of love that is very Lucretian in its language, even if the underlying idea is Petrarchan:

> Illius optatos suspiro cernere uultus,
> Quos Morpheus oculis subdidit ante meis:
> Iucundisque inhians simulacra retecta figuris,
> Materiae ductum, corpus ut umbra, sequor
>
> "Ad Iohannem Hagium", 175–8

> I yearn to see her face, the object of my desires, which Morpheus once set before my eyes: and gazing at images [*simulacra*] revealed in attractive forms, I pursue the lineaments of matter, as a shadow does the body.

This passage is partly about the pursuit of an ideal of transcendent beauty, but it also has a poetological dimension. In a recent work Colin Burrow has high-lighted the importance in Lucretius's poem of *simulacra*, shadows and spectral images as metaphors for *imitatio*, and suggested that this aspect of the work had a profound influence on Renaissance poetics.[152] Melissus's account of

---

149   Hock 2021.

150   A key passage is the following: "so in love Venus deludes lovers with *simulacra*, nor can bodies physically present satisfy them with looking, nor can they rub off anything with their hands from tender limbs as they wander at random all over the body" ("sic in amore Venus simulacris ludit amantis, / nec satiare queunt spectando corpora coram / nec manibus quicquam teneris abradere membris / possunt errantes incerti corpore toto", *De rerum natura* 4.1101–1104).

151   Hardie 2002: 150–163.

152   Burrow 2019: 112–119.

the creative process of writing love poetry is characterized by the language of *simulacra*, dreams and substanceless images. Earlier in the passage, Melissus writes of Lotichius that "he took pleasure in imitating the shadows [*umbras*] of the ancients";[153] and that when he set out to write elegy, the Muse Erato presented him an image of beauty to put into poetry. Melissus thus links the erotic pursuit of the imaginary object of desire to literary *imitatio*. Lotichius's mistress is a figment, he imitates shadows, but the poetry he creates from these insubstantial impulses is something solid and substantial: it is no "carmen inane". Melissus's account of the process of poetic creation, which bodies forth substance from what is without substance, thus further draws on the Lucretian language of the void that is constitutive of matter (the "inane" that is "in rebus", *DRN* 1.330).[154]

One other notable feature of Melissus's defence of love poetry is that he yokes his Petrarchan-Lucretian-Ficinian arguments to a separate set of arguments more attuned to Protestant views on marriage. He recognizes that love poetry does not only deal with the ideal and the abstract, and that love poets do not only sing a chaste Petrarchan love: physical love may be a valid subject for poetry insofar as it is validated by marriage and procreation.[155]

10   **Conjugal Love and Family**

Whereas married love had never been a very prominent theme of ancient Greek and Roman love poetry, except in the relatively restrictive form of the *epithalamium*,[156] Latin poets of the Christian era addressed it frequently, and devoted entire books of poems to its celebration.[157] One obvious reason for this is that views of the role and function of marriage in Greco-Roman societies differed in fundamental ways from the conception of it in Christian thought deriving from the writings of Saint Paul. Another is that the theme of conjugal love, given the absence of ancient models for first-person love poems about marriage, offered Neo-Latin poets new possibilities for innovation in the composition of thematically unified love poetry collections.

---

153   "Lotichio libuit priscorum imitarier umbras" ("Ad Iohannem Hagium", 93). On the collocation of *umbra* and *imitari* in Lucretius, see Burrow 2019: 113.

154   Cf. Burrow 2019: 117.

155   "Ad Iohannem Hagium", 59–65, and see Descoings 2009 for a discussion of the implicit parallels in Melissus's poem between conjugal procreation and poetic fecundity.

156   But see also Wasdin 2018 on the overlaps (or 'interdiscursivity') between ancient wedding poetry and love poetry.

157   Recent collective volumes on the topic: Galand & Nassichuk 2011; Lionetto 2021.

Roman love elegy generally eschewed marriage in the type of love relation-ship it depicted. Although fantasies of longing for a lasting relationship akin to marriage feature in Propertius and Tibullus, and marriage imagery is prom-inent (in ambiguous ways) in Catullus's Lesbia cycle, these fantasies never come to pass. Only in works situated at the limits of the elegiac genre do we find poems addressed by husbands to wives or wives to husbands: a couple of poems in Propertius Book 4; Ovid's *Heroides* and *Tristia*. The male persona of classical love elegy is more likely to express explicit opposition to marriage as a social institution and its role in perpetuating existing power structures. Propertius's lines at 2.7.5–10 put it most forcefully: "I'd sooner let this head be parted from my shoulders [than marry] ... Why should I breed sons for our country's Triumphs? / No soldier shall come from my bloodline."[158]

Neo-Latin love elegists likewise usually portrayed their love as extra-marital; and the relationship between the persona and the *puella* was often implicitly – sometimes explicitly – adulterous. The persona might also adopt more or less direct anti-marriage poses, but rarely expressed a critique as forceful as Prop. 2.7. The anti-conjugal dimension of Neo-Latin elegy drew in part on themes from satire and epigram (misogynistic portraits of shrewish wives, or repulsive, often elderly, husbands). Frequently it took the milder form of Tibullan-style yearning for a lost Golden Age in which love was free from constraint by social institutions like marriage. Pontano in the *Parthenopaeus* writes of mutual love liberated from social obligation in these terms.[159] Equally, though, in the pro-grammatic poem at the head of the first book of that collection, Pontano ima-gines that his love poetry is specifically for a readership of married lovers:

Legem versiculis dedere nostris
Aetas et male sobrius magister,
[...]
Vt molles, lepidi, leves, iocosi;
Quos uxor canat in sinu mariti,
Quos coniux legat in sinu puellae.
     Parthenopaeus 1.1.6–12

Youth and the scarcely sober master
have laid down the law for our little verses:

---

158 "nam citius paterer caput hoc discedere collo / quam possem nuptae perdere more faces [...] unde mihi patriis natos praebere triumphis? / nullus de nostro sanguine miles erit."
159 *Parthenopaeus* 2. 2; on which see Leroux 2021: 7–9, with discussion of other treatments of this theme in Neo-Latin elegy.

[...]
that they be soft, charming, light, playful, the kind of thing
that a wife croons in the embrace of her husband,
or a husband reads in the embrace of his bride.[160]

Perhaps surprisingly, the defence conventionally used to justify obscenity and illicit love in poetry[161] is used here by Pontano to claim that love poetry of a soft and sensual kind belongs to the domain of married love. Pontano has in mind Martial *Epig.* 1.35, which proposes an analogy between erotic epigrams and wedding songs or conjugal sex, but he goes further in imagining husbands and wives as the proper performers and audience for his poems. Indeed, he particularizes the notion in the second part of the poem by describing the erotic play of the married couple to whom he dedicates the book.[162] Thus even in Pontano's early poetry, in which the celebration of conjugal love has not yet become the central theme, marriage is already a key reference point. In the *Parthenopaeus*, he alludes on several occasions in particular to Catullus's wedding poems 61 and 62, and even expresses his literary debt to Catullus by comparing it to the gratitude a young bride owes her father for giving her in marriage to a beloved husband (*Parthen.* 1.19.31–36).[163]

Pontano developed the theme of married love in earnest in an elegiac collection written over a long period later in his career: *De amore coniugali.* Pontano from the outset explicitly situates the work in the framework of classical love elegy. In the first poem, he gives a detailed portrait of the personified Elegia, supplementing Ovid's description of her in *Amores* 3.1 with a divine genealogy and backstory of his own invention, and specifying that her native land is Umbria – birthplace of Propertius, and of Pontano himself. But it becomes clear in the course of this poem that this is a fundamental reconfiguration of the language and values of elegiac love. In it Elegia speaks in the role of *praeceptrix amoris* (love's teacher), but her lessons to girls are quite the opposite of those of Ovid in the *Ars amatoria*:

> Anne iuvet residem frustra duxisse iuventum
>   expertem grati credula coniugii?
> Quin potius laudanda fores, si coniuge caro,
>   si Veneris placidis ipsa fruare bonis.

---

160 Trans. by J. H. Gaisser. See Gaisser 2012: 179–180.
161 The reference is to the 'law of Catullus' (Cat. 16.5–8), on which see below, pp. 81–89.
162 On the significance of this move, see Gaisser 2019: 1343.
163 Nassichuk 2021: 10–13.

Ut sine aqua fluvius utque est sine frondibus arbor,
    ut sine sole dies, nox sine luminibus,
Sic turpis sine amore pari, sine coniuge lectus:
    deliciis ille est illecebrisque locus.
        De amore coniugali 1.1.109–116

Would you enjoy spending your youth in pointless idleness,
without part in agreeable matrimony,
credulous girl? If you should choose, instead, to take
enjoyment of the peaceful fruits of Venus,
and of your dearest spouse, why then you would win praise!
Just as a river without water's flow,
a tree without its leaves, a day without the sun,
a night without stars, so unlovely seems
a bed without harmonious love, without a spouse.[164]

In transforming Elegia into a *praeceptrix* of married love (and dressing her in the garb of a Roman matron), Pontano is remembering Statius *Silvae* 1.2, a poem in which Elegia is made over to mingle unnoticed in an epithalamic chorus for the statesman and elegiac poet Lucius Arruntius Stella. But Pontano's point is different: as Luke Roman puts it, "In Statius, an elegiac lover becomes a married man. In Pontano, a married man writes elegy."[165]

The version of love elegy created by Pontano must abandon many of the features of the love relationship that shaped the dynamics of ancient elegy. Most of the barriers that stood between the classical elegiac lover and his mistress – locked doors and guardians; jealous husbands, rivals and go-betweens; her demands for gifts in exchange for sex – necessarily dissolve in the context of a marriage relationship. But Pontano deftly retains and adapts other aspects to invest married love with something of the tension and eroticism of classical elegy.[166] He also interweaves the language of love elegy with ceremonial phrases from Renaissance wedding ritual and with allusions to contemporary nuptial oratory and treatises on marriage, meaning, according to the argument of Matteo Soranzo, that the collection should be read as an ideologically motivated intervention in response to new political developments in the court of Naples.[167]

---

164   Translation by Luke Roman (Pontano 2014: 10–11).
165   Pontano 2014: xvii–xviii.
166   Pontano 2014: xv–xvii.
167   Soranzo 2016: 47–70. Nassichuk 2021 also situates the work in its political context, connecting it in particular to Pontano's account of the ethical and civic functions of marriage in the prose treatise *De obedientia* (1490).

Pontano's collection celebrates not only married *eros*, but the love of parents for their children, a theme largely absent from Roman poetry. The second book of *De amore coniugali* concludes with a sequence of *naeniae* (lullabies) in elegiacs, composed by Pontano for his new-born son Lucio Francesco. Lullabies are not normally called love poems, but this innovative short collection most certainly does merit inclusion in the discussion, since Pontano is consciously adapting the language and idioms of elegiac and Catullan love poetry to the expression of parental affection.

After Pontano, married love was a theme often taken up by Neo-Latin love poets. Perhaps the best known – or at least the most frequently studied – example is Jean Salmon Macrin's *Epithalamiorum liber* (1531); first issued 1528 as *Carminum libellus*).[168] Despite its title, this work is not a collection of *epithalamia* in the proper sense of the word: it is a mixture of poems written in hendecasyllables, in Horatian metres, and one in elegiacs, mostly but not all addressed to the poet's wife 'Gelonis' (Guillone Boursault).

> Mellitas cithara Macrinus odas
> Flacci personat instar et pudicos
> mores coniugis optimae atque amores
> effert laudibus ...
>
> NICOLAS BOURBON, *Nugae* 196[169]

Macrin plays sweet odes on the cithara, just like Horace, and exalts with praise the modest life of his excellent wife, and his love for her.

Contemporary readers like Bourbon clearly wanted to see Salmon Macrin's 'Horatian' identity (and metrical virtuosity) as the determining influence on his love poems to Gelonis; but for the erotic dimension of the *Epithalamiorum liber* Catullus is the more important stylistic model. Bourbon highlights the "modest" ("pudicos") character of the poems' subject, in pointed contrast to the Catullan preference for poems that are "rather immodest" ("parum pudici", Cat. 16.8). But Salmon Macrin had opened his book with a programmatic poem in hendecasyllables fusing Horatian (*Carm.* 1.1) and Catullan (Cat. 16) intertexts, and suggesting that Catullan *licentia* and not Horatian stateliness would be the dominant note.

---

168   Ford 1997; Galand-Hallyn 1998 (and numerous other articles by Galand); Schumann 2009; Guillet-Laburthe 2011; with the editions Salmon Macrin 1998 and 2011.

169   Bourbon 2008: 468–470.

Dum carmen tibi nuptiale, proles
o Regum inclyta Caesarumque sanguis
Honorate, dico levesque nugas
volvi abs te nimis impudenter insto,
frontem exporrige comis ad iocosas
festi delicias Thalassionis.
Scriptorem argue nec procacitatis,
si quid legeris hic ineptiarum.
Nam legem tulit hanc Catullus olim,
princeps Hendecasyllabôn Catullus,
ut castus foret integerque vates,
vatis carmina non item, lepore
quae tum praecipue suo placerent
si essent mollicula at parum severa.
Nos legem sequimur Catullianam
Fescenninaque ludimus, Camoenae
Praefati veniam licentiori.

Epithalamiorum liber 1

I dedicate this wedding song to you, great offspring of kings, blood of the
Caesars, Honoratus, and I impudently give these slight scraps for your
perusal: smooth your forehead and kindly come to the amusements of
merry Thalassio. And do not accuse the author of effrontery if you read
anything foolish here. For Catullus once, Catullus the prince of the hendecasyllable, passed this law – that the poet be virtuous and pure, but
not the poet's songs, which seem especially smart and pleasant if they are
rather delicate and not too severe. I follow the law of Catullus, and trifle
with Fescinnine songs, apologizing in advance for my rather free Muse.

Like Pontano in the poem from the *Parthenopaeus* quoted above, Salmon
Macrin invokes the 'law of Catullus' in support of a poetic vision of married
love (notably replacing Catullus's "parum pudici" with "parum severa": cf.
Martial 1.35.1). He calls the collection a wedding song ("carmen nuptiale") and
mentions "Thalassio" (the Roman wedding god) and "Fescinnine songs" (the
Roman custom of bawdy songs sung at the wedding to ward off the evil eye).
All of these allusions point towards Catullus's own wedding poems (61 and 62),
which might lead the reader to expect the collection to consist of poetry in that
mode. In fact the poems that follow are of a quite different kind.

What we find instead is a sequence of first-person lyric poems celebrating the joys of conjugal love and home, drawing on various traditions of love

poetry – Horatian, Catullan, Petrarchan and elegiac. Like Pontano, Salmon Macrin has adjusted the conventions and idioms of elegiac love to the marriage situation, and has reconfigured the elegiac structure of the lover's separation from his beloved to express a different set of values. Overlaying the elegiac notion of the lover's exclusion is the thematic opposition of public life and domestic *otium*:

> Illa o quando aderit dies, Geloni,
> cum dices mihi blandulo susurro
> affusa in teneris meis lacertis:
> Te, mi vir, volupe est venire salvum
> ut mecum hic placida quiete felix
> penses taedia et asperos labores,
> quos annis prope quindecim tulisti,
> regem huc dum sequeris vagantem et illuc.
>> *Epithalamiorum liber* 9.1–8

O when will that day come, Guillone, when you'll say to me in a flirtatious whisper, melting in my tender arms: 'How delightful is your safe homecoming, my husband, to be happy here with me in restful repose, and compensate for the tedium and harsh tasks that you have borne for almost fifteen years while you followed the king travelling all over the realm.'

It is the rigours of service at the itinerant royal court that delay and frustrate the fulfilment of the persona's desires, which are for the pleasures of family, home and the countryside of his native Loudun, as well as for erotic satisfaction.

The apparent mismatch between the title and content of Salmon Macrin's *Epithalamiorum liber* should not lead us to neglect the fact that innumerable *epithalamia* were indeed written by Neo-Latin poets, both for public occasions in celebration of the weddings of rulers and patrons, and more personal poems for weddings of their friends and fellow humanists. The main classical models were Catullus 61, 62 and 64, Statius *Silvae* 1.2, and Claudian's *Epithalamium Honorii et Mariae*. Probably the best known Neo-Latin example is Johannes Secundus's Catullan *epithalamium* beginning "Hora suavicula, et voluptuosa", which devotes the majority of its 145 lines to sensual descriptions of the wedding night (but does not appear to be connected to a specific wedding occasion). The extended analysis of the *epithalamium* form in Scaliger's *Poetices* (1561) seems to have led to a revival of the form especially among northern European poets, who were no doubt influenced too by the fact that the practice and function of marriage were being fundamentally reconceptualized in

Protestant thought. Daniel Heinsius and Hugo Grotius (1583–1645) composed many examples of nuptial verse on classical models.[170] Friedrich Taubmann (1565–1613) produced numerous Anacreontic *epithalamia* – an innovation that won a large audience – including, most famously, an extraordinary baroque confection written for the wedding of Paulus Melissus Schede.[171]

11 Obscenity

One does not have to look very hard to find among the productions of Neo-Latin love poets examples of writing that is lurid, sexually obscene and even pornographic. Equally, there is a strong trend of anti-obscene writing. Its arguments were sometimes motivated by moral or aesthetic considerations; sometimes they were clearly a proxy for wider disputes, primarily religious ones; and sometimes they served the purpose of mere character assassination.

Those Neo-Latin poets who found themselves having to justify their use of obscenity in love poetry, or who wished to head off potential objections in advance, could cite a number of classical models and arguments in their defence. Chief among these was Catullus 16, a poem which Julia Gaisser has called "the founding and programmatic text of erotic Latin lyric and epigram in the Renaissance".[172] The key lines were not its shockingly violent opening and conclusion, but the formulation that came to be known as the *lex catulliana* (the 'law of Catullus'): "It is right for a devoted poet to be pure himself, but his verses need not be. They in the end have wit and charm only if they are delicate and immodest" (Cat. 16.5–8).[173] To this could be added a familiar grouping of commonplaces: what the emperor Hadrian wrote of the poet Voconius, "You were wanton in verse, modest in mind" (Hadrian 2); what Ovid wrote from exile to Augustus, "Believe me, my morals differ from my poetry. My life is modest, my Muse playful" (*Tristia* 2.353–354); and Martial 1.4.8, "My page is wanton, my life is upright". At the base of these arguments are two interrelated ethical

---

170 Van Dam 2009: 104–112; and Tufte 1970: 87–93 on Neo-Latin *epithalamia* generally. I note here also the existence of an interesting collection by Nathan Chytraeus, *Amorum coniugalium libri III* (1579), which does not yet seem to have attracted much scholarly attention.

171 Tilg 2014: 187–190. The following sample, from an interminable passage describing the beauty of the bride is quoted by Tilg: "Argenteum labellum / Corallinum labellum, / Sapphirinum labellum, / Beryllinum labellum, / Topazinum labellum, / Hiacinthinum labellum, / Smaragdinum labellum, / Labellulumque bellum ..."

172 Gaisser 2019: 1326.

173 For discussion of early modern uses of this theme, see Gaisser 1993: 208–11, 224–33; Gaisser 2019; Ford 2011.

and literary principles: first, the idea of the separation of a poet's life and work, and second, the notion of *decorum* of literary genre: that language and themes should be fitted to what is appropriate for the genre in which one writes (Ovid, *Remedia amoris* 361–398).

Antonio Beccadelli was the author of one of the first – and one of the filthiest – Neo-Latin collections in imitation of Martial, of the *Priapeia*, and, to a much lesser extent, of Catullus: the *Hermaphroditus* (1425). Beccadelli wrote in his opening poem to Cosimo de' Medici:

> Hac quoque parte sequor doctos veteresque poetas,
> quos etiam lusus composuisse liquet,
> quos et perspicuum est vitam vixisse pudicam,
> si fuit obsceni plena tabella ioci.
> Id latet ignavum volgus, cui nulla priores
> visere, sed ventri dedita cura fuit;
> cuius et hos lusus nostros inscitia carpet.
> *Hermaphroditus* 1.1.5–10

> And in this I follow the example of the learned poets of old,
> Who, it is clear, composed trifles
> And, it is evident, lived modest lives,
> Even if their pages were full of obscene jokes.
> The lazy crowd fails to notice this, who have no care to look to the ancients
> But whose only care has been given to their belly.
> Their ignorance will pick at my trifles too:
> So be it – the learned will not reproach me.[174]

Beccadelli returns several times to this defence in the course of the collection. Its point is not really to insist seriously upon the principle of the separation of a poet's life and work – to warn against what modern readers might call the biographical fallacy. It is, rather, a glib expression of unconcern about the censorious opinions of dull readers. Those who are in the know – learned, Latin literate, men who know their Martial and Catullus – will cope; the rest can go hang. In the event, Beccadelli's *Hermaphroditus* did come in for plenty of opprobrium, but it was also – initially, at least – admired by learned humanists who got the point.[175] Guarino Guarini (1374–1460), in a letter of praise which

---

174   Beccadelli 2010: 6–7. Translation by H. Parker.
175   See O' Connor 1997; Parker in Beccadelli 2010: xiii–xvi; and Coppini 2020 for the view that the angry polemic sparked by the *Hermaphroditus* was really more motivated by social and professional rivalry than by genuine moral outrage.

he would later retract, approved of Beccadelli's artistry, to which, he said, it is no detriment that "it smacks of jokes, playfulness and something a little wanton";[176] of course he quoted Catullus 16.5–9 in support. Poggio Bracciolini (1380–1459), although he cautioned Beccadelli against over-stretching a point, also approved, and made fun of the stupidity and childishness of the critics: after all, "we all play around with words"[177] (the 'we' being learned, sophisticated, Latin literate men). The general notion that you could get away with more in Latin than in the vernacular persisted for much of the period. Latin composition offered a fenced-off space where complicity with readers who were sufficiently cultured granted greater licence in poetic expression, which might not be permitted for works at risk of reaching the *ignavum vulgus* – or women. As Jelle Koopmans puts it, "language deterritorializes the obscene".[178]

The notion of a restricted readership is clearly important, but one of the conceits of love poetry in the Catullan-elegiac vein is that the intended audience for the poetry is female as much as it is male. A wrinkle in Beccadelli's defence was that he did not envisage an exclusively male readership for his "obscene jokes". At *Hermaphroditus* 2.23 the poet begs his friend Galeazzo to track down a copy of Catullus for him so that he can "gratify" his mistress with it ("ut possim dominae moriger esse mihi"). She is lustful ("lasciva"), he explains, and is in the habit of reading "the tender poets", among whom she has a particular liking for Catullus.[179] This is a reader who wants Catullus for the thrills; but there is still, in this poem, a sense that the reading of him is justified by the exclusivity conferred by the fact that he is a "learned" poet – *doctus*, the adjective used here of Catullus by Beccadelli, was the epithet most readily associated with him.

The idea that reading poetry was in itself an erotic act, that love poetry was a way for the male poet to sexually satisfy his female reader, was in part what motivated many of the panicked condemnations. It was also a witty conceit beloved of poets well read in Martial and Catullus. Martial's well known epigram 1.35 answered criticisms by asserting that books of poetry, like husbands with their wives, cannot give pleasure without a cock ("non possunt sine mentula placere"), and that that "law" laid down (*sc.* by Catullus) dictates that humorous poems cannot be enjoyable unless they arouse ("ne possint, nisi pruriant, iuvare"). Secundus, in his *Basia*, found a way to further contort

176 "quia iocos, lasciviam et petulcum aliquid sapiat" (*Guarini in Hermaphroditon iudicium* (February 1426) in: Beccadelli 2010: 2).

177 "iocamur saepe verbis, utimur facetiis et salibus quae si eadem redderemus gesta corporis, diceremur merito insani" (Poggio to Beccadelli, April/May 1426, in Beccadelli 2010: 138).

178 Koopmans 2021.

179 Beccadelli 2010: 88.

Martial's already heavily ironized argument. The premise of *Basia* 12 is the inverse of Martial 1.35: the critics are mistaken if they think there is anything in his poetry that cannot be read by a schoolmaster to his pupils. There are no "carmina mentulata" (poems with a cock) here. But Secundus then imagines that the passing mention of this word has suddenly revived the attention of the crowd of *matronae* and *puellae*, their prudishness now unmasked as prurience. The punchline:

> quanto castior est Neaera nostra,
> quae certe sine mentula libellum
> mavult, quam sine mentula poetam.
>> *Basia* 12.16–18

> how much more chaste is my Neaera,
> who certainly prefers a book without a cock
> to a poet without a cock.

The twists and turns of this poem are quite typical of the mood of Secundus's love poetry as a whole, which is characterized (as Alex Wong puts it) by "an attitude of ironic disingenuousness which almost always has to do with questions of sexuality".[180] What is noteworthy is that the argument that emerges, through the veil of disingenuousness, is one that disposes of the need to posit a 'chaste' life for the poet, and even speaks approvingly of female sexual desire.

The frowning and pursed-lipped readers imagined by Beccadelli and Secundus were conventional foils for their barbs, but there was in reality (it goes without saying) no shortage of such censorious readers, even within the confraternity of sophisticated and classically educated humanist poets. A rallying point for them was Mantuan's *Contra poetas impudice loquentes* (or *scribentes*) (1487; first printed Bologna 1489), an attack on writers of obscene poetry, targeted at imitators of Catullus and Martial such as Beccadelli and Pontano, and more generally at those writers whom the Carmelite poet saw as promoters of Epicureanism and paganism. Mantuan's mission was to repeal the *lex catulliana*:

> Vita decet sacros et pagina casta poetas,
>> Castus enim vatum spiritus atque sacer.
> Si proba vita tibi lascivaque pagina, multos
>> Efficis incestos in Veneremque trahis.

---

180   Wong 2017: 95.

Verba movent animos, oris lascivia pectus
　　Pulsat et in venas semina mortis agit.
　　　　Contra poetas 19–24

It is right that sacred poets be pure both in life and on the page, for pure
and sacred is the inspiration of bards. If you have a upright life and wanton page, you are making many readers impure and betraying them to
Venus. Words move minds, wantonness of speech stirs the heart and
spreads the seeds of death in the veins.

Mantuan draws up a series of binary distinctions throughout the poem, in the
first place between the pure 'gold' of true poetic eloquence and the filth and
dirt of erotic poetry, and later between what is weighty and serious ("gravis")
and what is light and frivolous ("levis"). The danger of poetry that is "levis" is in
the effect it has on others, not necessarily the effect it has on the poet himself.
Mantuan wants to curb licence in poetry not because the words themselves are
light and frivolous, but because words do have weight and so can easily lead
readers into error. As Jodocus Badius Ascensius (1462–1535) put it in his commentary on the poem (which he wrote for the impressionable audience of the
boys he was teaching at a school in Lyon in the 1490s): "more serious and more
dreadful than the sin we commit by ourselves is the sin we commit through
others" ("gravius autem et formidandum magis est peccatum quod per alios
quam per nos patramur").[181]

　　As Gaisser points out, Mantuan picks up the term 'castus' from Catullus 16,
but by it he means something different from what Catullus had meant.[182] In
that poem, Catullus was responding in an exaggerated way to his friends Furius
and Aurelius who had criticized his poems for being too soft and unmanly
("molliculi"); to be 'castus' in that context had to do with avoiding the stigma
of passive sexuality.[183] Mantuan the Carmelite mostly understands 'castitas' in
the more general sense of sexual purity, and neo-Catullan erotic poetry is the
main target he has in his sights in the poem. But he also attacks any poetry that
declares itself to be trifling or light, and at the climax of the poem he draws
up a list of suitable themes for poetry (cosmological, philosophical and divine
subjects): serious, weighty themes that aim at the cultivation of virtue rather
than the fleeting fame that is the motivation of frivolous love poets.

181　Badius 1492: 135ʳ.
182　Gaisser 2012: 183–4.
183　For more on how Renaissance commentators read these lines, see Ford 2011 and Wong
　　　2017: 88–91.

The *Amores* (1542) of Simon Lemnius (*c.*1511–1550) has gained a certain notoriety as a scandalous piece of pornography, although judgements of his poems and indeed of his character were perhaps informed more by knowledge of Lemnius's scurrilous dispute with Martin Luther than by a close reading of the love poems themselves.[184] What distinguishes Lemnius treatment of sex (which is not, we should note, the sole focus of the poems in the *Amores*) from the epigrams of a Beccadelli or even a Secundus – many of which are extremely and imaginatively obscene – and explains why they have been described as 'pornography' rather than accepted as examples of 'learned obscenity' is that they do not use references to sexual organs and sex acts for the purpose of satire, invective, or shock-value – or even simply for the sake of a joke for those in the know. They are, instead, pornographic in the modern sense of the word, in that they focus on "the direct usage of sexual gratification, with an emphasis on male 'users'".[185] Thus they present extended descriptions of sex, often framed by luxurious descriptions of landscape and the domestic environment, with a focus on the male persona's own performance and gratification. Although it is possible to identify ancient and Neo-Latin models for some of the sexual vocabulary used by Lemnius (for example, when the poet repeatedly informs the reader of the insertion of his penis "to the seventh rib", alluding to *Priapeia* 6 ("ad costam tibi septimam recondam")), Mundt is probably right to suggest that Lemnius's overall approach to the representation of sex in the *Amores* is largely without precedent in ancient or Neo-Latin love poetry.[186]

In his epigram "To the reader" introducing the collection, Lemnius disdains the usual excuse of an upright life giving the lie to the wanton page:

> Non haec lascivae tibi sunt epigrammata musae,
> > Crede mihi nulli carmina nostra nocent.
> Hic tantum teneros miseri deflemus amores,
> > Continet eventus pagina tota meos.
> Si quid erit forsan, de me tu scripta putabis,
> > Ista Venus nostra est, iste Cupido meus.
> Haec legat et tetricus, legat haec et fronte serenus,
> > Haec legat et Curius, Fabritiusque simul.

These poems I present to you are not epigrams of a wanton Muse; believe me, my poems harm nobody. Here I only sadly lament tender loves; every

---

184   Mundt 1991: 519–20; and see Mundt's edition: Lemnius 1988.
185   This definition is from Enenkel 2014: 487.
186   Mundt 1991: 525–6.

page contains things that happened to me. If anything comes of it, you will consider that these writings are about me. This is *my* Venus, and this is *my* Cupid. Let stern men read them, and let those of glad countenance read them too: Curius and Fabricius both may read them.

Lemnius insists on the autobiographical truth of his poems – although any reader marvelling at the extraordinary athleticism of the sex acts described therein might be inclined to doubt him. But there is ambiguity in lines 5–6. Should we supply quote marks to line 6 and read Lemnius as saying that readers will look at the poems about his experiences and say to themselves: 'this is also *my* experience of love'? Such a sentiment would be a conventional elegiac one, in the manner of Ovid *Amores* 2.1.7–10;[187] but it would not quite make sense in the context of the poem. Or is line 6 to be read as a continuation of direct speech in the persona's own voice? The point would then be that Lemnius claims the erotic experiences documented in the book as his own and his alone. The idea then seems to be that the poems cannot harm the reader, since anything immoral or obscene in them belongs fully to the author: he takes full responsibility for them, so the reader can escape being implicated, and read them with impunity.

The *lex catulliana* was a very flexible proposition, and it lent itself to different and even opposing applications. (Even in Catullus's own formulation it was sufficiently ambiguous to be open to several different interpretations.) It was, we might say, all case law and not statute. The terms on which the argument was made shifted, and later writers found that it did not stand up when exposed to scrutiny. Théodore de Bèze felt that he had to exercise greater caution in invoking it, even in the context of his argument that his love poetry was fictional and bore no relation to his life. He avoids appealing directly to the *lex catulliana*, and indeed rhetorically dismisses it (in a section of his argument designed to expose the hypocrisy of his critics):

> Age igitur illa, quod tamen absit, vera esse concedamus: nec illa veteris
>   poetae in re simili defensio quicquam valeat
> *Lasciva est nobis pagina, vita proba est.*
> (Nam certe, ut et ipse aliquando cecini,

---

187 "atque aliquis iuvenum, quo nunc ego, saucius arcu / agnoscat flammae conscia signa suae / miratusque diu 'quo' dicat, 'ab indice doctus / composuit casus iste poeta meos?'" ("And may some youth, wounded by the same bow that has now wounded me, recognize the tell-tale signs of his own passion, and marvelling at length say: 'what informer taught this poet to write of my own misfortunes?'").

Quae fecisse nefas, fingere facta nefas)
quae haec tamen istorum impudentia est, illud ipsum in Beza tam grav-
iter accusare, quod in suis omnibus ultro ferant?[188]

Go on then, let us concede that those things are – God forbid! – true,
and say that that defence of the ancient poet in a similar matter has no
force: "My page is wanton, my life upright". For surely as I myself have said
elsewhere: "What is wrong to have done, is wrong to imagine done"; still,
what impudence they have to charge Bèze so seriously with that same
thing that they would gladly tolerate in all of their own [Catholic poets].

Sins of the imagination are just as culpable as sinful acts. We are a long way
here from the pre-Reformation arguments: even Mantuan never went that far.
And in a poem "Against the hooded Beza-bashers" (*In cucullatos Bezastigas*),
included in the 1569 edition of his *Poemata*, he again implied that the ancient
'law' should no longer be used as a defence. His accusers, he wrote, charge him
with sins on the basis of what he wrote in his fictional poems, even though
they commit such sins for real; they are hypocrites, but the charge itself may
be just:

Et merito, siquidem hos demum haec fabrilia fabros,
    Seria seu fuerint, seu simulata, decent.

And rightly so, since these tools, *whether real or imagined*, only befit these
craftsmen.[189]

Bèze's point here is that if he committed sins in his writing (which he admits),
it was because of the corrupting influence of the culture in which he spent his
youth – the very culture of his Catholic accusers. We are, again, very far here
from the glib unconcern that characterized uses of the *lex catulliana* in earlier
Neo-Latin literature.

In post-Reformation cultures the grounds for a moral defence of erotic
poetry had shifted substantially. The question of how to justify the use of erotic
themes in poetry (and indeed the notion that they required justification at all)
became a more urgent concern, particularly for Protestant poets. For example, when Johannes Hagius Francus wrote the biography of his friend Petrus
Lotichius Secundus (printed 1586), he felt compelled to address the problem

---

188   Aubert et al. 1980: 92.
189   Emphasis mine. Trans. by Kirk Summers in Bèze 2002: xxxii.

of Lotichius's love poetry.[190] That it should even be considered a problem at all seems surprising: love poems made up only a very small part of Lotichius's elegiac oeuvre, and there is nothing remotely obscene in any of them. But Hagius viewed the very existence of these love poems as a nagging difficulty that needed to be disposed of, a knotty problem to be solved ("is scrupulus eximendus superest, ac dissolvendus nodus"). To make his case, Hagius did not rely at all on the law of the separation of a poet's life and work; indeed, he took it as fact that the mistresses Lotichius addressed in his love poems were real women loved by him. Instead he argued, first, that the love of beauty is the privilege of poets: the contemplation and explication of the celestial and terrestrial visible forms of all that is beautiful in the world is proper to the poetic art. Second, that Lotichius in fact loved all those women chastely, and without any hint of impropriety (and consecutively, nor concurrently!). Third, that having chosen to write about love (since nothing human was alien to him), he had a poetic duty to write in a way fitting his theme, which was for him a therapeutic diversion from the troubles of life. That Hagius felt the need to deploy so many arguments in defence of Lotichius's rather innocuous poems of love is partly a reflection of the changed context in which he wrote, and partly a function of the generic requirements of literary biography and Hagius's aim to secure Lotichius's reputation as the greatest poet of his age.

12   Homosexuality

Doubtless the majority of erotic lyric and epigrammatic poems from Greek antiquity concern homosexual and pederastic love rather than heterosexual love. The Roman poets provided models for heterosexual love poetry, but even the most insistently heterosexual of the Roman genres – love elegy – also encompassed homoerotic poems (Tibullus's Marathus), and Catullus was known for his poems of love to the youth Juventius as well as for his Lesbia cycle. Neo-Latin poetry tended to suppress homosexual elements, but did not completely erase them.

The presence of same-sex love in Greek lyric and epigram or in Tibullus, Catullus and Martial did not necessarily pose problems for early modern authors writing in contexts where it could simply be ignored or passed over in silence: these texts, after all, did not have a place in the curricula of schools.

---

190   Hagius's *Vita Lotichii* is printed in full in the second volume of Burmann's edition (Lotichius 1754), with the section on Lotichius's love poems at pp. 135–8. For a general discussion of the biography, see Weiss 1984.

Virgil, on the other hand, most certainly did. Virgil's second *Eclogue*, which concerns homoerotic desire and opens with the lines "The shepherd Corydon was burning with love for handsome Alexis, his own master's darling" ("formosum pastor Corydon ardebat Alexin, / delicias domini") could of course be quietly omitted from selections read in the schoolroom, but it could hardly be expurgated entirely from the innumerable editions and translations of the works of the most widely read poet of all. Erasmus, in his *De ratione studii*, advised teachers to take the line that has over the centuries so frequently been used to erase same-sex love: essentially, that Corydon and Alexis were 'just good friends'.[191] The second *Eclogue* was widely imitated in Neo-Latin pastoral poetry on love themes, but usually reframed in terms of heterosexual love relationships – as in Sannazaro's *Ecloga Piscatoria* 2, discussed above.[192]

Two Neo-Latin poetry collections notorious in their time for their pederastic content have attracted critical attention in recent years: Beccadelli's *Hermaphroditus* and Pacifico Massimi's *Hecatelegium*. In the controversy about the *Hermaphroditus* the most savage attacks on Beccadelli focused on the pederastic poems (see for example the two epigrams by Lorenzo Valla); and Becadelli in his eventual recantation (*c.*1435) mentioned specifically his shame at having written of acts "which nature shuns" ("quos natura fugit").[193]

Even humanists who expressed general approval of Beccadelli's poetry stopped short of endorsing his arguments in defence of his use of pederastic themes. Beccadelli, reacting to a letter from Poggio which had sounded a note of mild reproof amid general praise for the *Hermaphroditus*, had set out an expansive argument based on the ancient defences of erotic poetry, and citing as precedents numerous poets and authors who wrote works which he saw as being of the same type as his. Poggio in a second letter warned Beccadelli against calling as witnesses authors who would not actually support his case, and gave special attention to Beccadelli's defence of his use of the pederastic theme. Beccadelli, drawing on Apuleius *Apologia* 9, cited Plato as the author of numerous seductive poems to boys, and added the example of the pseudo-Platonic epigram about the soul-kiss, quoting in full the Latin version found in Aulus Gellius beginning "As I kiss my boy [*meum puellum*] with half-opened lips" (discussed above, pp. 70–72). Poggio for his part admitted that the Greeks had the freedom to say and make up whatever they wanted ("liberta[s] dicendi fingendique quae vellent"), but they were writing at a time when loving boys was forbidden neither by custom or by law ("quod tum neque

---

191   Grafton 1994: 38; Hollewand 2021: 71–2.
192   And see Fredericksen 2015: 428–429.
193   Valla's epigrams: Beccadelli 2010: 189–191. The recantation: Beccadelli 2010: 125–127.

moribus neque legibus prohibebatur"). Those things were permitted in Plato's time, but not in ours.[194]

The *Quattrocento* mediators of Plato's philosophy could easily reject the attribution of the pederastic epigrams to Plato as false; but the central status of same-sex love in Plato's philosophical works was still a challenge for them. Early humanists such as Leonardo Bruni suppressed or modified it in translation; Ficino retained the idea that love between males is superior to love of a man for a woman, but specified that this higher love should be chaste.[195]

Scholarship for most of the modern era discreetly averted its gaze from the *Hecatelegium* (1489) of Pacifico Massimi (*c.*1400–1506), but this work has in recent years attracted a growing number of readers.[196] Massimi himself clearly anticipated both types of response, as he wrote in an amusingly provocative epigram *Ad lectorem*:

> Lector si sapis haud legas libellum,
> sed uites, fugiasque, respuasque,
> ut pestem rabidam, grauemque morbum.
> Sin, ne dixeris: 'Haud poeta dixit'.
> Fies pessimus e bono, maloque
> longe pessimus. Hoc poeta dixit.
> Perstas tu tamen, et uidere curas.
> Nosces quod facis et quod ipse scripsi.

> Reader, if you have any sense don't read this book; avoid it, shun it, spit it out like a rabid plague or a horrible disease. Otherwise, don't say 'The poet didn't tell me'. If you're good, it will make you the worst, if bad, the worst of the worst. The poet has told you this. But you persist, and you still want to see. You'll soon realize what you're doing, and what I have written

Massimi's "One Hundred Elegies" is a work of extraordinary length and variety, encompassing conventional love elegies addressed to a *puella* named Martia, invective and satirical verses, and even poems on cosmographical and philosophical themes. But the aspect of the work that has most engaged modern

---

194   The text of this correspondence can be found in Beccadelli 2010: 56–58; 112–124; 130–138.
195   Kraye 1994; Reeser 2016.
196   Massimi 1986 and, for the second *Hecatelegium* (!), Massimi 2008 (editions by Juliette Desjardins); and see now also Massimi 2021 (Alessandro Bettoni's edition of *Hecatelegium* I) with further bibliography there.

readers is Massimi's frank treatment of same-sex love, which has led some to
view him as a major figure in gay history and to read his poems as documentary evidence of the homosexual experience in Renaissance Italy.[197] That some
modern readers have been inclined to take Massimi's poems as autobiographical must be partly because of the unusual character of many of these elegies:
Massimi frequently adopts a confessional, yet provocative and defiantly transgressive, register of a kind that seems tonally quite different from the autobiographical pretence we normally find in love elegy. In *Hecatelegium* 1.9, for
example, the persona addresses to a certain Paulinus an account of his life
including (15–18) his youthful experience of sexual abuse at the hands of a pederastic tutor to whom his parents had ill-advisedly entrusted him. Elsewhere
Massimi writes in the persona of a pederast himself (7.3), or jokes that the
reason he is called 'Pacificus' is that "nature made me a *pathicus*" ("quod me
pathicum fecit natura" 2.8.73).

Massimi's *Hecatelegium* certainly merits further scholarly attention, not
necessarily for its documentary value, but for its complex and multifaceted
performative dimension, and the extraordinary richness of its poetic discourse,
which interweaves numerous allusions to Catullus, Martial, the *Priapea*, the
Roman elegists and the satirists, and the Greek Anthology with popular prov-
erbs and everyday speech.

Massimi and Beccadelli were both attacked in their lifetimes as sodomites,
but so were numerous other Neo-Latin poets whose works contained little or
nothing as provocative as what they wrote. Such attacks could be motivated by
petty intellectual and social rivalries, or be part of a context of wider religious
and political conflicts. It was common for accusations of sodomy to be paired
with a charge of heresy, as when in 1554 in Toulouse Marc-Antoine Muret was
condemned and burned in effigy "pour être huguenot et sodomiste".[198] Muret's
Odes 2 has sometimes been cited as a text that motivated the accusation. The
poem, "On the departure of Daniel Schleicher, the sweetest son by far" (*In
discessu Danielis Schleicheri, filii longe dulcissimi*), tenderly laments the departure (not death) of a male companion, possibly one of Muret's students:

> Nunquamne posthac conspiciam tuos,
> Schleichere, vultus? cur igitur moror
> Nec tristis invisaeque vitae
> Fila ferox inimica rumpo?
>   Iam iam valete, o gaudia et o ioci,

---

197   Dall'Orto 2002.
198   On Muret's conviction, see Ferguson 2008: 121–2.

Et quicquid antehac dulce fuit mihi;
Venite iam fletus perennes
Perpetuique venite planctus.

Odes 2.21–8

Never after this will I see
your face, Schleicher? Why then do I delay
and not bravely break the cruel threads
of this sad and hated life?
Now farewell, joys and laughter,
and whatever before this was sweet to me;
welcome, endless weeping,
welcome constant tears.[199]

It is not certain that this poem actually was a pretext for the accusations, but later opponents of Muret cited it as such. The more classically minded of them might have picked up on Muret's self-comparison to Orpheus in lines 9–12, and recalled that Orpheus was the fabled inventor of pederasty. The actual reasons for the accusations are obscure, but there is no doubt that Muret's conviction was grist to the mill of religious polemic, particularly after Muret had fled to Rome and had, in 1576, taken holy orders. Théodore de Bèze who, as we have seen, had faced similar accusations on the basis of his Latin poetry, wrote an epitaph unsparing in condemnation of Muret the Roman Catholic: "For in what city should a sodomite have rather lived? And in what city should a wicked man have more fittingly died?"[200]

13 Love's Transformations; Metamorphosis and Mannerism

The vast importance of Ovid's *Metamorphoses* as a source of inspiration for poets and for visual and plastic artists in the early modern period has been

---

199 Trans. by Summers in Muret 2006: 190–1; and see Summers' discussion of the sodomy charges in the commentary, 204–5.

200 "Gallia quod peperit, pepulit quod Gallia monstrum: / Quem Veneti profugum non potuere pati, / Muretum esse sibi civem iussere Quirites, / Et tumulo extinctum composuere suo, / Vivere nam potius qua debuit urbe cynaedus? / Impius et quanam dignius urbe mori?" (The monster that France brought forth, then drove out; whom Venice could not endure in his exile – Muret – the Romans approved as one of their own, and now that he is dead, buried him in one of their tombs. For in what city should a sodomite have rather lived? And in what city should a wicked man have more fittingly died?).

much studied. The poem, being a narrative mythological epic bookended by cosmological and philosophical musings on the theme of change, might seem to fall outside the scope of the present study. But its influence on Neo-Latin love lyric was considerable. The most popular sections of the poem have perhaps always been those episodes from the early books in which Ovid, influenced by Hellenistic and neoteric *epyllia*, is chiefly concerned with erotic themes. Ovid's version of epic is, moreover, profoundly shaped by his preoccupations as an elegiac love poet, both in terms of its thematic focus and in his liking for antithetical and paradoxical formulations that touch upon deeper psychological truths.

The *Metamorphoses* was not the only classical source for early modern love poets writing of erotic transformations. Greek and Roman love lyric and epigram provided numerous models for lovers' fantasies of self-transformation. The Greek Anthology contains several poems in which the speakers imagine themselves transformed into a rose, or the wind, or an apple, or evoke the transformations of Zeus into gold, a bull or a swan. Anacreontic 22, a poem in which the speaker wishes to be transformed into objects possessed or worn by his beloved (a mirror, a cloak, water, myrrh, a ribbon, a pearl, and a sandal), was popular with Renaissance translators and imitators.[201] Models in Roman love elegy include Ovid *Amores* 2.15, an erotic fantasy in which the persona imagines himself transformed into a ring, and the shapeshifter Vertumnus, the emblematic figure of Propertius Book 4. The theme of erotic metamorphosis was occasionally a feature of early Neo-Latin love elegy: Basinio's *Cyris*, as we have seen, presents a persona especially obsessed with textual transformations. An important model was Petrarch's *canzone delle metamorfosi* (*Canz.* 23), in which the long sequence of metamorphoses of the lyric persona – all allusions to episodes from Ovid's *Metamorphoses* – are expressions of the lover's suffering and mental distress, and ultimately the possibility of transcendence.

Nicolas Brizard, the poet mentioned above in the context of Petrarch translation, composed a sequence of Latin hexameter poems entitled *Metamorphoses amoris* (1556). Its subject is not 'love's transformations' in the sense of changes suffered or fantasized by lovers; it proposes instead a series of allegorical portraits of the metamorphoses of the love god himself into "varias figuras", including – among around 60 other guises – a mirror, a parrot, an owl, death, a bubble, the Lernaean Hydra, and finally, into nothing ("in nihilum").[202]

Brizard's treatment of the theme exemplifies the tendency that we find in many poets of this period to amplify and develop conventional themes to the

---

201   Rosenmayer 2002: 415–419.
202   On this work, which had a French translation by François Habert (1561), see Nassichuk 2015.

point of exhaustion. The idea of perpetual transformation and of the infinite reversibility of a poetic proposition appealed to humanists trained to argue *in utramque partem* and to poets accustomed to developing set themes *ad infinitum*. The love elegies of Vincent Fabricius (1612–1667) apply this mentality to the thematic structure of the classical elegiac book. In book 2 of his *Elegiae*, Fabricius abstracts the themes and images of love elegy and sets them in an antithetical structure, with successive poems arguing first one, then the opposite proposition about love: that lovers should be bold – that lovers should be timid; that the absence of one's lover is a good thing – that a lover's absence is bad; that lovers are like kings – that lovers are like prisoners or slaves; and so on. We see elements of this structure already in Ovid's *Amores*, in which successive poems reverse the position of the previous one; but the point here is to abstract the argument to the level of the discourse itself. The mental contortions and reversals that characterize the thought processes of the elegiac poet-lover now take place as a second-order disputation over the images, metaphors and themes of love poetry. This is a culmination of the mannerist poetic tendency, which is based in variation, elaboration and distortion of the topoi and images of the tradition with which it engages, and ultimately a distancing and abstraction of those themes.

One of the reasons for the prominence of the metamorphic theme in Neo-Latin love elegy relates to the conceptual basis of the classical genre itself, which is characterized by antithesis, instability and dynamism. The persona of classical elegy restlessly takes up opposing positions, hesitates to assume a definitive guise. He is a self divided, plagued by uncertainty and delusions, at odds with his socio-cultural milieu and with himself. The macabre obsessions of Propertius, his depiction of the *furor* of love, his sudden reversals and oscillations between extremes;[203] Ovid's delight in paradox and illusion, in the specular and the spectacular, his inversions and elaborations of conventional images and themes: all of these features were amplified and magnified in the work of Neo-Latin imitators. They reached their fullest expression in the later part of the sixteenth century as Neo-Latin love elegy met vernacular mannerism and neo-Petrarchism,[204] and lovers' metamorphoses assumed more extravagant guises.

Janus Dousa again provides an illustrative case. Among the poems appended by Scriverius to his *Cupidines libri duo* are several translations into Latin elegiacs of French sonnets by the mannerist poet Philippe Desportes (1546–1606).

203 On this aspect of Propertian elegy see Gibson 2007: 43–69.
204 On metamorphosis as a central preoccupation of mannerist and baroque vernacular love lyric, see e.g. Mathieu-Castellani 1980 & 1981.

They are part of a conscious and explicit attempt to align Latin love elegy with vernacular mannerism. One of them begins:

> Non tot tamque nouos habitus assumpsit & ora
> Pomonae sponsus, Carpathiusve senex,
> Quam subito in formas varias mutamur amantes,
> Nosque Venus miras induit in facies.[205]

> The husband of Pomona, and the old Carpathian, never assumed so many and such different appearances and countenances as we lovers do when we are instantly transformed into various forms and Venus clothes us in strange guises.

There follows a description of the lover's transformations into a stag, a swan, a flower, and others. The Desportes poem (*Amours de Diane* 1.34) is itself clearly based on Petrarch's *canzone delle metamorfosi*, but in the course of its transformations from Italian into French into Latin it has accumulated some intriguing elaborations. The conclusion:

> Unde novus fons emicui, per lumina colans
> Quod reliquum in nobis omne liquoris erat.
> Scilicet ut putri lacrymarum ex imbre renascens,
> Mutarem nomen rursus, ut ante, meum:
> Et, qui fons fueram, fierem Salamandra repente.
> Sic itaque in medio vivitur igne mihi.
> Quid superest, nisi uti fiam vox denique, perpes
> Quae canat, et laudes personet, Ida, tuas?

> Then I sprang forth as a fountain, draining through my eyes all of the water that was left in me. Of course this was so that I might change my name again, as before, reborn from the putrid liquid of my tears; and become, who had been a fountain, suddenly a salamander. So my life is lived in the midst of fire. What is left, but that I become, in the end, a voice, forever singing and echoing praise of you, Ida?

The famous Desportes poem translated here by Dousa is in many ways the *exemple type* of the mannerist style of French poetry. Its theme of transformation is reflected in the rapid succession of images and motifs that evoke

---

205   Dousa 1609: 571–2.

a series of allusive relations – primarily Petrarchan, ultimately leading back to Ovid's *Metamorphoses* – which never settle into coherency or unity, never resolve into focus; indeed, they resist resolution, even at the moment of the final *pointe*. The poem revels in the strain it places on the conventional metaphors of love, such as the fountain that drains itself through its eyes. Dousa's Latin reproduces and amplifies these features, and it strives for striking formal effects, for example in the alliteration and assonance of "Et, qui fons fueram, fierem Salamandra repente". Dousa also introduces elements to make the translation work as a Latin love elegy. Quite apart from the fact he inserts at the end the name of his own elegiac *puella*, Ida, thus establishing the continuity of these poems with his love elegy books proper, he introduces two figures at the start that are not in Desportes's poem: the husband of Pomona (Vertumnus) and the old Carpathian (Proteus). The former evokes Propertius 4.2 – and the translation as a whole resembles that poem of Propertius in other ways too, syntactically and structurally – and the latter is a precise verbal echo of Ovid *Amores* 2.15.10, the elegy in which the poet-lover fantasizes his own transformation into a ring which is somehow also a phallus.

Thus vernacular mannerism gets reclaimed or reabsorbed into the classicizing discourse of love elegy. The inclusion of the Desportes translations as part of Dousa's own love elegy collection, which itself exploits many of their themes and images, foregrounds the continuities between them. This is a reperformance of the French mannerist sonnet as Latin elegy.

Another striking example of what I would call Neo-Latin mannerism is the Latin version of Pierre de Ronsard's famous sonnet *Je voudroy bien richement jaunissant* by François de Thoor (Thorius, b.1525–d. before 1601).[206] The translation reproduces more or less faithfully the sequence of ideas in Ronsard's sonnet – the lover's wish to be transformed into a golden rain (alluding to Jupiter's seduction of Danaë), a bull (Jupiter and Europa), and Narcissus – but its verbal textures, its word choices and poetic effects are mannered in the extreme:

> Vellem ego flaventi liquefactus membra metallo
> Auripluas fluere in guttas, mictumque meae me
> Phyllidis in gremium pretioso fundere nimbo
> Languidulos illi quum somnus inivit ocellos.

---

206 See Ford 2013: 174–183; 186–193 on Latin versions of Ronsard's love poetry by Jean Dorat, Paulus Melissus, Martial Monier and François de Thoor; and Prescott 2016: 167–8 for the text of this Latin poem and a brief discussion.

I wish that I could be liquified to golden metal, and for my limbs to flow in drops of golden rain, and for me to pour from a precious cloud, spurting into the lap of my Phyllis, when sleep has entered her tired little eyes.

The elaborations in the Latin, partly there to fill out the metre, also have the effect of amplifying the sexual meanings of the lover's fantasy, and tipping it into the realm of the bizarre. "mictum" in line 2, if it is the supine of *mingere* (to piss), is tonally jarring,[207] but there is a certain logic to it in the context – and the expression "mictum … in gremium" echoes Cat. 67.29–30.[208] The primary meaning of *mingo* was 'urinate', but it also meant 'ejaculate', as in the Catullan example.[209] *gremium* could mean 'vagina' and *membra* in the plural could mean 'penis'. The overall effect is of a poetic fantasy that is both over-embellished and rather sordid.

Metamorphosis is central to the expression of elegiac love in the *Elegiarum libri quattuor* (1584) of a much better poet, Jan Kochanowski (1530–1584).[210] He uses it as a way both to explore the psychology of erotic desire, and to figure the instability of his elegiac poetic discourse itself. In his opening poem (1.1), an atypical *recusatio*, the lover fantasizes about role-playing as an Amphion, a Linus or a Hercules. In 1.6 he compares his beloved Lydia to those nymphs for whom Jupiter transformed into gold, a bull, and a bird (echoing *Gr. Anth.* v.125, which Kochanowski also translated in his epigrammatic collection *Foricoenia*). In 1.10 he imagines Lydia disguising herself as a man to come to him, and remembers Jupiter taking the form of Diana to seduce Callisto, who was then transformed into a bear (Ovid, *Met.* 2.405–531). In Kochanowski's elegiac vision, metamorphosis is linked to erotic fantasy but also to the desire of the frustrated lover to become something other than himself, to escape the confines of his own self-torturing mind. This mood is expressed most forcefully in 2.3, which is both Ovidian and Catullan in its representation of the agonizing self-alienation of the lover:

> Quid me tam variis torques, Amor improbe, curis
>   Et rapidi huc illuc turbinis instar agis?
> [...]

---

207   It could be "mistum" (= mixtum); see Prescott 2016: 167 n.13.
208   "egregium narras mira pietate parentem, qui ipse sui gnati minxerit in gremium."
209   Adams 1990: 142.
210   For this collection see the edition by Cabras (Kochanowski 2019) and Urban-Godziek 2005: 134–159 and 2015.

Nunc me in diversas raptari sentio partes
  Et furit in venis iraque, amorque meis.
[...]
Ibo, sed facile est fugere urbem et limina nota,
  At quis tam pernix, se quoque ut effugiat?
    Elegiae 2.1.1–2; 29–30; 39–40[211]

Why, wicked Amor, do you contort me with such diverse anxieties, and drive me hither and thither, like a tearing whirlwind? [...] Now I feel myself pulled apart in different directions, and both anger and love rage in my veins. [...] I'll go, but it is easy to flee the city and familiar bounds: but who could be so quick as to get away even from himself?

Much of this is traditional enough – and these lines contain echoes of Strozzi and Lucretius as well as of Ovid and Catullus[212] – but there is something distinctive about the prominence of themes like this, and the intensity with which they were expressed, in the Latin love poetry of the later sixteenth and early seventeenth centuries. This period sees northern European poets and theorists transform the genre of Latin love elegy itself; they conceptualized Latin elegy as a form uniquely capable of depicting the violent and unstable emotional states associated with love; indeed, they argued that this was fundamentally what elegy was *for*.

Valens Acidalius (1567–1595), in a treatise on the true nature and definition of elegiac poetry (*Oratio de vera carminis Elegiaci natura et constitutione*, first published posthumously in 1606), wrote:

Ut si quis affectus describere conetur amatorios (sumamus enim hoc exemplum, ut Elegiae maxime proprium) de ipsis primo affectibus erit cogitandum. Eos ut vehementes, ita mobiles et inconstantes, uti turbidos, sic praecipites, saepe sibiipsis adversantes contrariosque deprehendet. Quid iam? Poteritne Poeta istam affectuum varietatem et inconstantiam ipso Euripo aestuosiorem uniformi versuum tractu, aequali numerorum serie, pari syllabarum dimensione, quasi in pictura, ut oportebat, repraesentare? Profecto non poterit, si rei naturae parem velit (quod omnino velle et efficere posse debet) orationis naturam et esse et videri.[213]

---

211   Kochanowski 2019: 312–3.
212   See Cabras's commentary in Kochanowski 2019: 313–324.
213   Acidalius 1606: 386.

So if one tries to describe love's passions (let us take this example, since it is especially relevant to Elegy) it will first be necessary to think carefully about the passions themselves. He will observe that they are so violent, so unstable and inconstant, so disordered, so sudden, and often at odds with themselves and self-contradictory. What then? Could a poet represent, as if in a picture (as he should), that variety and inconstancy of the passions, more agitated than the very strait of Euripus, in a uniform passage of verse, in an even metrical sequence, in an equal measure of syllables? Clearly he could not, if he would like the nature of the language to be and to appear equal to the nature of the thing itself (something that he absolutely must want and be able to achieve).

This is a passage about *decorum* and imitative harmony, such as one might find in any number of humanist treatises on poetics, but the view expressed here is in direct opposition to dominant humanist ideas about elegiac versification. In making this argument, Acidalius is closely following Janus Dousa (indeed, much of this passage is directly copied from the latter's *Praecidanea pro Albio Tibullo*)[214] to argue against a conception of love elegy that associated it with smoothness and fluency. The earlier theorists – Dousa targets Johannes Murmellius (c.1480–1517) and Georgius Sabinus (1508–1560) in particular – had set out numerous metrical prescriptions for composition in elegiacs, mainly based on the practice of Ovid; their preferred metaphor for the elegiac couplet was that the that of the free flowing river. But Dousa and Acidalius championed the use in love poetry of disruptive metrical features which had previously been judged either to be faults of versification, or to be reserved for use in funerary elegy, such as the frequent use of spondees in the fifth foot of the hexameter, repeated use of hiatus, sense units running over the pentameter to the next hexameter (*enjambement*), and pentameters ending in a polysyllabic word.

For these theorists and poets, love was not an experience that could be expressed in easily flowing regular verse, but one so unstable, disorderly and violently at odds with itself that its poetic expression must at times evoke discord and unease. The poetic form proper to the expression of love was not the flowing river but the raging torrent or the dangerous, unpredictable strait; or, in a comparison Acidalius also makes, the painted landscape whose pleasant aspect is disrupted by the intrusion of ruins and jutting deformities.[215] The

---

214   Dousa 1582: 60.

215   Acidalius 1606: 414. Acidalius borrows this comparison in part from the *Poetices* of Julius Caesar Scaliger, who criticizes the excess of such defects in painting and poetry. In Acidalius these supposed defects have become an example of something desirable.

presence of such defects, excrescences and incongruencies in love poetry is desirable not only because it is essential to the accurate portrayal of conflicting emotions, but because it has an aesthetic value of its own. Latin love elegy was entering its baroque phase.

14   Conclusion

Those who frequent already lyricized themes draw on vast and deep resources of memory and tradition to create their art. Latin love poets of the early modern period were not merely passive receivers of influences from elsewhere; their works were energized by dynamic interactions with other texts and cultures; they varied and innovated forms and themes; they engaged in complex negotiations to define and situate their work in relation to different poetic genres, different languages, and different historical periods.

To speak of the Latin love poetry of the early modern period is to attempt to encompass a capacious and immensely varied textual universe. This poetry was produced throughout Europe, over a long period of time, in numerous genres and styles, and with varying degrees of orientation towards classical, mediaeval and contemporary vernacular traditions. It had a transnational dimension, to be sure, but it also varied according to local conditions and the local audiences it aimed to reach. Viewed from a distance, the traditions of Neo-Latin love poetry appear remarkably stable over a long chronological span – the gravitational pull of the classical models tended to stabilize its trajectories – but on closer examination, it is possible to observe change over time. Genres and forms underwent modifications, as poets reinterpreted the classical models and reconfigured their responses to them, and interacted with vernacular traditions of love lyric.

Research into Neo-Latin love poetry has benefitted in recent years from a notable shift of scholarly attention towards the poetic output of major humanist authors. Marc-Antoine Muret is now just as likely to be studied as a poet as he is as a scholar; and it is fair to say that interest in the work of Cristoforo Landino has in the last decade or so turned decisively from his prose œuvre to his poetry. It is, of course, the work of producing editions that provides the foundation and impetus for further research – the kind of work that is both arduous and, unfortunately, often insufficiently incentivized by institutional research agendas and funding regimes. A great deal of progress has been made in publishing editions of works by major authors, the best of them being *bona fide* critical editions furnished with modern language translations and commentaries. Many of the best recent editions of this kind have been of works by northern European – particularly French – poets, but it is still true to say that the Italian *Quattrocento* poets have, to date, been better served than poets from beyond the Alps and from the later part of period. My own wish-list of modern editions would include in first place the *Cupidines* of Janus Dousa, followed by the love elegies of Paulus Melissus Schede and the *Monobiblos* of Daniel Heinsius. The future is perhaps in 'born-digital' online editions; but there is also great value for researchers in reliably transcribed printed editions made available online, such as those provided by the websites "Poeti d'Italia in lingua latina" and "CAMENA" (mainly for German Neo-Latin poets).[216]

The volume and variety of Latin love poetry make it amenable to a very broad range of scholarly approaches and methodologies running the whole gamut of the discipline of literary studies. If recent criticism is still largely characterized by traditional modes of reading Neo-Latin poetry grounded in the study of genre and *imitatio*, it is certainly the case that many of the assumptions underpinning such approaches have been revised and modified.

Although genre still is – and for good reasons – the principal instrument that scholars use to bring works of Neo-Latin love poetry into focus, and still provides the dominant frameworks for interpreting them, nevertheless research has now developed a richer and more nuanced sense of how generic composition worked in Neo-Latin poetry. Clearly early modern conceptions of the genres of Latin poetry were never identical with classical ones, however much humanists wished to believe they were; and they were contested, and changed over time. Equally, classical genre conceptions had never been identical with themselves (so to speak), particularly in the domain of Roman love poetry, since its canonical authors – poets of the Augustan age thoroughly versed in Alexandrian and neoteric poetics – saw generic experimentation and the mixing of genres as an essential part of the aesthetic they cultivated. Neo-Latin poets picked up these tendencies from their Roman models, and their conceptions of genre were shaped by interactions with non-classical poetic traditions too, as recent work on the symbiosis or dynamics of vernacular and Neo-Latin poetry has shown.

The study of *imitatio* in Neo-Latin love poetry is likewise now less narrowly focused on a small canon of classical models, and is no longer conceived in linear, unidirectional terms. Editors and critics are increasingly likely to take notice of the presence of other Neo-Latin and vernacular texts as models for imitation, as the greatly expanded scope of the *apparatus fontium* in some recent editions shows. Although it is clearly the case that Neo-Latin love poets did explicitly privilege classical Roman and Greek models in their poetological

---

216   "Poeti d'Italia": <http://mizar.unive.it/poetiditalia/public/>. "CAMENA": <http://mateo .uni-mannheim.de/camenahtdocs/camenapoem_e.html>.

statements, the status of the models themselves was not fixed, and could change over time. Different versions of the classical came into and fell out of favour; vernacular models could be elevated to 'classic' status; models viewed at one time as mediaeval or late antique could become classical; and so on. One reception model that I find helpful in understanding these processes is the 'Transformation' methodology (developed at the Humboldt University in Berlin, as set out in the 2019 book *Beyond Reception*),[217] which posits that instances of reception work simultaneously to modify the 'sphere of reception' and to construe or construct 'the sphere of reference' and that the two processes are mutually implicated in one another, a reciprocity which is given the name 'allelopoeisis'.

In addition to reception theory, I would highlight two other (intertwined) strands that have been prominent in recent research on early modern Latin love poetry. First, analyses that focus on its metapoetic dimension have shown how poets used the discourses of love poetry to reflect on its status as literature, to position it in relation to different traditions, and to work through aesthetic, ethical and religious arguments. Second, socio-cultural approaches have taken us beyond the naïve biographicism characteristic of much of the earlier scholarship to show how Neo-Latin love poetry played a major role in self-fashioning and the formation of identities both local and transnational. The rhetorical strategies, poses and personas love poets adopted in their works were constructed upon the long-established foundations of past traditions, but they took shape in response to the conditions of the present: the literary, social and political allegiances that motivated and oriented their work.

There is also potential for more theoretically informed work to extend in other directions. For example, both feminist and psychoanalytical approaches have featured strongly in research on classical love poetry in recent decades, but have been much less prominent in Neo-Latin research. The gender aspect has been less studied, as has the subversive and counter-cultural dimension of Neo-Latin love poetry.

As more editions become available and more studies of individual works are published, there is increasing potential for more broad-based studies taking up both synchronic and diachronic perspectives. It would, in particular, be beneficial to have more ambitious comparative studies spanning different national and local contexts and communities of poets and readers. Equally welcome would be studies charting the shifting conceptions of love and its codes of representation in Latin poetry against the background of the conflicts, upheavals and discoveries that characterized the period.

---

217 Bergemann et al. 2019.

Bibliography

Primary[218]
I Tatti Renaissance Library Series

Ariosto, Lodovico. 2018. *Latin Poetry*. Translated by Dennis Looney and D. Mark Possanza. Cambridge, MA: Harvard University Press.

Beccadelli, Antonio. 2010. *The Hermaphrodite*. Translated by Holt N. Parker. Cambridge, MA: Harvard University Press.

Bembo, Pietro. 2005. *Lyric Poetry; Etna*. Translated by Mary P. Chatfield. Cambridge, MA: Harvard University Press.

Filelfo, Francesco. 2009. *Odes*. Translated by Diana Maury Robin. Cambridge, MA: Harvard University Press.

Landino, Cristoforo. 2008. *Poems*. Translated by Mary P. Chatfield. Cambridge, MA: Harvard University Press.

Marrasio, Giovanni. 2016. *Angelinetum and Other Poems*. Translated by Mary P. Chatfield. Cambridge, MA: Harvard University Press.

Marullus, Michael. 2012. *Poems*. Translated by Charles Fantazzi. 54. Cambridge, MA: Harvard University Press.

Poliziano, Angelo. 2018. *Greek and Latin Poetry*. Translated by Peter E. Knox. Cambridge, MA: Harvard University Press.

Pontano, Giovanni Gioviano. 2006. *Baiae*. Translated by Rodney G. Dennis. Cambridge, MA: Harvard University Press.

Pontano, Giovanni Gioviano. 2014. *On Married Love ; Eridanus*. Translated by Luke Roman. Cambridge, MA: Harvard University Press.

Sannazaro, Jacopo. 2009. *Latin Poetry*. Translated by Michael C. J. Putnam. Cambridge, MA: Harvard University Press.

Verino, Ugolino. 2016. *Fiammetta; Paradise*. Translated by Allan M. Wilson. Cambridge, MA: Harvard University Press.

Other Modern Editions

Aldegati, Marcantonio. 1980. *Marcantonio Aldegati: poeta latino del quattrocento*. Edited by Guglielmo Bottari. Palermo: Il Vespro.

---

218   Modern editions are listed first, preferring those with translations into English or other modern languages where available. Where no modern edition exists or is easily accessible, I have listed the early printed edition(s) consulted by me. Reliable texts of several of the Italian Neo-Latin collections can be accessed through the online resource "Poeti d'Italia in lingua latina" <http://mizar.unive.it/poetiditalia/public/>.

Andrelinus, Publius Faustus. 1982. *Amores sive Livia*. Edited by Godelieve Tournoy-Thoen. Brussels: Paleis der Academiën.

Basini, Basinio. 1925. *Le poesie liriche di Basinio (Isottaeus, Cyris, Carmina varia)*. Edited by Ferruccio Ferri. Turin: G. Chiantore.

Bèze, Théodore de. 2002. *A View from the Palatine: The* Iuvenilia *of Théodore De Bèze*. Edited by Kirk M. Summers. Tempe, AZ: Center for Medieval and Renaissance Studies.

Bologni, Girolamo. 1993. *Candidae libri tres*. Edited by Caterina Griffante. Venice: Istituto Veneto di Scienze, Lettere ed Arti.

Borghini, Caterina. 1826. *Due Elegie latine di Caterina Borghini di Pisa: Unde novo radiat lux conspicienda sereno? (Oculi nigri); Vos ego, caerulei, mea lux, meus insignis ocelli (Oculi caerulei), pubblicati per Le Nozze Crescini-Meneghini*. Padua: Tipografia del Seminario.

Borghini, Caterina. 2001. "Elegiae." Edited by Allegra Alacevich. *Lo Stracciafoglio: Rassegna Semestrale di Italianistica* 4: 47–55.

Bourbon, Nicolas. 2008. *"Nugae" (Bagatelles) 1533*. Edited by Sylvie Laigneau-Fontaine. Geneva: Droz.

Boyd, Mark Alexander. 2010. *Ovidius redivivus: die* Epistulae heroides *des Mark Alexander Boyd: Edition, Ubersetzung und Kommentar der Briefe Atalanta Meleagro (1), Eurydice Orpheo (6), Philomela Tereo (9), Venus Adoni (15)*. Edited by Carolin Ritter. Hildesheim: Olms.

Braccesi, Alessandro. 1943. *Carmina*. Edited by Alessandro Perosa. Florence: Bibliopolis.

Buonaccorsi, Filippo ('Callimachus'). 1981. *Carmina*. Edited by Francisco Sica. Naples: Fratelli Conte.

Cambini, C. Aurelio. 1965. "The Poems of C. Aurelius Cambinius." Edited by John F. C. Richards. *Studies in the Renaissance* 12: 73–109.

Celtis, Konrad. 1934. *Quattuor libri Amorum secundum quattuor latera Germmaniae*. Edited by Felicitas Pindter. Leipzig: Teubner [also available in an online edition (Brepols, 2010: http://clt.brepolis.net/)].

Cleofilo, Francesco Ottavio. 2003. *Julia*. Edited by Mauro De Nichilo. Messina: Centro interdipartimentale di studi umanistici.

Du Bellay, Joachim. 1984. *Oeuvres poétiques 7. Oeuvres latines: Poemata*. Edited by Geneviève Demerson. Paris: Nizet.

Ducher, Gilbert. 2015. *Épigrammes*. Edited by Sylvie Laigneau-Fontaine and Catherine Langlois-Pézeret. Paris: Champion.

Ficino, Marsilio. 2002. *Commentaire sur le Banquet de Platon, de l'amour = Commentarium in Convivium Platonis, de amore*. Edited by Pierre Laurens. Paris: Belles Lettres.

Flaminio, Marcantonio. 1993. *Carmina*. Edited by Massimo Scorsone. Turin: Edizioni RES.

Folengo, Nicodemo. 1990. *Carmina.* Edited by Carlo Cordié and Alessandro Perosa. Pisa: Scuola normale superiore di Pisa.

Genesio, Fabrizio. 1970. "Elegiarum libellus." In *Nuovi documenti per la storia del rinascimento,* edited by Tammaro De Marinis and Alessandro Perosa, 147–66. Florence: Leo S. Olschki.

Hessus, Helius Eobanus. 2008. *The Poetic Works of Helius Eobanus Hessus Vol. 2: Journeyman Years, 1509–1514.* Edited by Harry Vredeveld. Tempe, AZ: Arizona Center for Medieval and Renaissance Studies.

Kochanowski, Jan. 2019. *Elegiarum Libri Quattuor: Edizione Critica Commentata.* Edited by Francesco Cabras. Florence: Firenze University Press.

Lemnius, Simon. 1988. *Amorum libri IV.* Edited by Lothar Mundt. Bern: Peter Lang.

Mantuanus, Baptista. 1989. *Adulescentia: The Eclogues of Mantuan.* Translated by Lee Piepho. 1st ed. New York: Garland.

Marrasio, Giovanni. 1976. *Johannis Marrasii Angelinetum et carmina varia.* Edited by Gianvito Resta. Palermo: Centro di studi filologici e linguistici siciliani.

Marullus, Michael. 1995. *Hymnes naturels.* Edited by Jacques Chomarat. Geneva: Droz.

Massimi, Pacifico. 1986. *Les cent élégies: Hecatelegium, Florence 1489.* Edited by Juliette Desjardins. Grenoble: ELLUG, Université Stendhal.

Massimi, Pacifico. 2008. *Les cent nouvelles élégies: deuxième Hecatelegium.* Edited by Juliette Desjardins. Paris: Belles lettres.

Massimi, Pacifico. 2021. *Hecatelegium I.* Edited by Alessandro Bettoni. Bologna: Patron Editore.

Melissus Schede, Paulus. n.d. "Paulus Melissus Schede: The English Poetry (1586)." Edited by Dana F. Sutton. Accessed April 29, 2022. <http://www.philological.bham.ac.uk/schede/>.

Molza, Francesco Maria. 1999. *Elegiae et alia.* Edited by Massimo Scorsone and Rossana Sodano. Turin: Res.

Muret, Marc-Antoine. 2006. *The* Juvenilia *of Marc-Antoine Muret.* Edited by Kirk M. Summers. Columbus: Ohio State University Press.

Muret, Marc-Antoine. 2009. *Juvenilia.* Edited by Virginie Leroux. Geneva: Droz.

Naldi, Naldo. 1934. *Elegiarum libri III ad Laurentium Medicen.* Edited by László Juhász. Leipzig: Teubner.

Naldi, Naldo. 1974. *Bucolica, Volaterrais, Hastiludium, Carmina varia.* Edited by W. L. Grant. Florence: In aedibus Leonis S. Olschki.

Piccolomini, Aeneas Silvius. 1994. *Carmina.* Edited by Adrianus van Heck. Vatican City: Biblioteca Apostolica Vaticana.

Piccolomini, Aeneas Silvius. 2003. *Œuvres érotiques.* Edited by Frédéric Duval. Miroir du Moyen Age. Turnhout: Brepols.

Pontano, Giovanni. 1902. *Carmina.* Edited by Benedetto Soldati. Florence: G. Barbèra.

Salmon Macrin, Jean. 1998. *Epithalames & odes*. Edited by Georges Soubeille. Paris: Champion.

Salmon Macrin, Jean. 2011. *Salmon Macrins Gedichtsammlungen von 1528 bis 1534. Edition mit Wortindex*. Edited by Marie-Françoise Schumann. Münster: Lit.

Sannazaro, Jacopo. 1914. *The Piscatory Eclogues*. Edited by Wilfred Pirt Mustard. Baltimore: Johns Hopkins Press.

Sannazaro, Jacopo. 1995. *Le ecloghe pescatorie*. Edited by Stelio Maria Martini. Salerno: Elea.

Secundus, Johannes. 2000. *The Amatory Elegies of Johannes Secundus*. Edited by Paul Murgatroyd. Leiden: Brill.

Secundus, Johannes. 2005. *Oeuvres complètes. Tome 1: Basiorum liber et odarum liber*. 97. Paris: Champion.

Strozzi, Tito Vespasiano. 1916. *Tito Vespasiano Strozzi poesie latine tratte dall'aldina e confronte coi codici*. Edited by Anita Della Guardia. Modena: Blondi & Parmeggiani.

Early Modern Editions

Acidalius, Valens. 1606. *Epistolarum Centuria I, cui accesserunt: (I) Epistola apologetica ad clariss. virum Iacobum Monavium. (II) Oratio de vera carminis elegiaci natura et constitutione*. Hanau: Typis Wechelianis.

Angeriano, Girolamo. 1512. *Erotopaignion*. Florence: P. Giunta.

Arduenna, Remaclus. 1513. *Amorum libri*. Paris: J. Badius.

Badius Ascensius, Jodocus. 1492. *Silvae morales*. Lyon: J. Trechsel.

Barth, Caspar von. 1607. *Casp. Barthii iuvenilia: Silvarum liber I; Sermonum liber I; Elegiarum lib. III; Lyricorum lib. I; Epigrammatum lib. I; Iamborum purorum lib. III; Eunapius in vita Proaeresii*. Wittenberg: L. Seuberlich.

Barth, Caspar von. 1612. *Casp. Barthii Amabilium Libri IV. Anacreonte modimperante decantati*. Typis Willerianis: Hanau.

Barth, Caspar von. 1613. *Amphitheatrum gratiarum, libris XV, Anacreonte modimperante constitutum*. Hanau.

Bayle, Pierre. 1697. *Dictionnaire historique et critique: Tome second, première partie*. Rotterdam: Reinier Leers.

Beroaldo, Filippo. 1487. *Commentarii in Propertium*. Bologna: F. de Benedictis for B. Hectoris.

Beroaldo, Filippo. 1491. *Orationes et carmina*. Bologna: F. de Benedictis for B. Hectoris.

Bèze, Théodore de. 1573. *Tractationes theologicae*. Vol. 2. Geneva: E. Vignon.

Bèze, Théodore de. 1599. *Theodori Bezae Vezelii Poemata varia: sylvae, elegiae, epitaphia epigrammata, icones, emblemata ...* Geneva: Stoer.

Blyenburgius, Damasus, ed. 1600. *Veneres Blyenburgicæ sive Amorum hortus*. Dordrecht: Isaac Caninus.

Bonnefons, Jean. 1587. *Pancharis*. Paris: A. L'Angelier.

Borghini, Caterina. 1756. "Elegiae." In *Arcadum Carmina: Pars altera*, 96–100. Rome: G. & F. de Rossi.

Brizard, Nicolas. 1556. *Metamorphoses amoris: Quibus adiectae sunt Elegiae amatoriae*. Paris: Maurice Menier.

Campano, Giannantonio. 1495. *Opera omnia*. Rome: E. Silber.

Campion, Thomas. 1595. *Poemata*. London: Richard Field.

Conti, Natale. 1550. *De horis liber unus ; eiusdem De anno libri quatuor ; Myrmico-myamachiae libri quatuor ; Amatoriarum elegiarum libri duo ; eiusdem Elegiae sex*. Venice: Per Fratres de Nicolinis de Sabio impressores apostolicos.

D'Espence, Claude. 1564. *Sacrarum Heroidum liber*. Paris: F. Morel.

Dousa, Janus. 1569. *Iani Douzae a Noortvvyck Epigrammatum lib. II. Satyrae II. Elegorum lib. I. Silvarum lib. II*. Antwerp: Gulielmus Silvius.

Dousa, Janus. 1582. *Praecidanea pro Albio Tibullo*. Antwerp: Plantin.

Dousa, Janus. 1609. *Poemata pleraque selecta*. Edited by Petrus Scriverius. Leiden: T. Basson.

Fabricius, Vincentius. 1685. *Orationes civiles [et] poemata*. Frankfurt: J. A. Plener.

Flaminio, Marcantonio. 1569. *Les Divines Poésies de Marc Antoine Flaminius, contenant diverses prières, méditations, hymnes et actions de grâce à Dieu, mises en françois, avec le Latin respondant l'un à l'autre, avec plusieurs sonnets et cantiques ou chansons spirituelles pour louer Dieu. Traduction de Anne de Marquetz*. Translated by Anne de Marquets. Paris: N. Chesneau.

[pseudo-] Gallus. 1501. *Cornelii Galli fragmenta*. Venice: B. Vitali.

[pseudo-] Gallus. 1588. *Asinii* [sic] *Cornelii Galli Elegia, nunc primum e tenebris eruta ab Aldo Manuccio. Eiusdem epigrammata tria*. Florence: G. Marescotti for A. Manutius.

Gallutius, Tarquinius. 1621. *Virgilianae vindicationes, et commentarii tres de tragoedia, comoedia, elegia*. Rome: A. Zannetti.

Heinsius, Daniel. 1603. *D. Heinsii Elegiarum. lib. III. Monobiblos Sylvæ, etc*. Leiden: J. Maire.

Heinsius, Daniel. 1621. *D. H. Poemata emendata ... et aucta ... Editio quarta*. Leiden: Elzevier.

Hosschius, Sidronius. 1656. *Elegiarum libri sex*. Antwerp: Plantin.

Lernutius, Janus. 1614. *Iani Lernutii Initia, Basia, Ocelli & alia Poemata*. Leiden: L. Elzevier.

Lotichius Secundus, Petrus. 1563. *Poemata Petri Lotichii Secundi Solitariensis*. Leipzig: in officina Voegeliana.

Lotichius Secundus, Petrus. 1754. *Petri Lotichii Secundi Solitariensis Poemata omnia quotquot reperiri potuerunt, editis auctiora et longe emendatora*. Edited by Petrus Burmannus Secundus. 2 vols. Amsterdam: Schouten.

Mantuanus, Baptista. 1489. *Contra poetas impudice loquentes*. Bologna: F. de Benedictis.

Melissus, Paulus. 1574. *Melissi Schediasmata poetica*. Frankfurt: G. Corvinus.

Melissus, Paulus. 1583. *P. Melissi ... Elegia ad Iohannem Hagium ... : amorem divinitus esse ingeneratum in hominibus*. Nuremberg.

Melissus, Paulus. 1586. *Melissi Schediasmata poetica: secundo edita multo auctiora*. 3 vols. Paris: Arnould Sittart.

Molza, Tarquinia. 1750. *Opuscoli inediti di Tarquinia Molza modenese con alcune poesie dell'istessa quasi tutte per l'addietro stampate, ma ora la prima volta raccolte, e poste insieme*. Bergamo: Pietro Lancellotti.

Monier, Martial. 1573. *Martialis Monerii Lemovicis Epigrammata, Elegiæ, et Odæ*. Bordeaux: S. Millanges.

Muret, Marc-Antoine, ed. 1554. *Catullus, et in eum commentarius M. Antonij Mureti*. Venice: P. Manutius.

Navagero, Andrea. 1530. *Andreae Naugerii Orationes duae, carminaque nonnulla*. Venice: J. Tacuinus.

Pentolini, Francesco Clodoveo Maria. 1776. *Le donne illustri: canti dieci*. Vol. 1. 2 vols. Livorno: V. Falorni.

Periander, Aegidius, ed. 1567. *Horti tres Amoris*. 3 vols. Frankfurt: Feyrabend & Huterus.

Sarbiewski, Maciej Kazimierz. 1632. *Lyricorum libri IV: Epodon Lib. unus alterque epigrammatum*. Antwerp: Plantin.

Scaliger, Julius Caesar. 1561. *Poetices libri septem*. Lyon: A. Vincent.

Scaliger, Julius Caesar. 1574. *Poemata*. Geneva: J. Stoer.

Vulstekius, Dionysius. 1612. *D. V.... Elegiarum et Epigrammatum Liber*. Middelburg.

Secondary

Albanese, Gabriella. 1999. "« Civitas Veneris »: Percorsi dell'elegia umanistica intorno a Piccolomini." In *Poesia umanistica latina in distici elegiaci: atti del convegno internazionale, Assisi, 15–17 maggio 1998*, edited by Giuseppe Catanzaro and Francesco Santucci, 125–64. Assisi: Accademia Properziana del Subasio di Assisi.

Aubert, Hippolyte, Alain Dufour, Claire Chimelli, and Béatrice Nicollier, eds. 1980. *Correspondance de Théodore de Bèze: Tome X (1569)*. Geneva: Droz.

Auhagen, Ulrike. 2008. "Marullus – ein 'Catullus pudicus' (Epigr. 1, 2)." In *Michael Marullus: ein Grieche als Renaissancedichter in Italien*, edited by Eckart Schäfer and Eckhart Lefèvre, 57–66. Tübingen: Narr.

Auhagen, Ulrike, and Eckart Schäfer, eds. 2001. *Lotichius und die römische Elegie*. Tübingen: Narr.

Baca, Albert R. 1972. "Propertian Elements in the *Cinthia* of Aeneas Silvius Piccolomini." *The Classical Journal* 67 (3): 221–26.

Baier, Thomas, ed. 2003. *Pontano und Catull*. Tübingen: Narr.

Balsamo, Jean, and Perrine Galand-Hallyn, eds. 2000. *La poétique de Jean Second et son influence au XVIᵉ siècle: actes du colloque organisé à Paris les 6 et 7 février 1998*. Paris: Belles lettres.

Beleggia, Barbara. 2006. "Echi Petrarcheschi negli *Eroticon libri* di Tito Vespesiano Strozzi." In *Il Petrarchismo: un modello di poesia per l'Europa.*, edited by Floriana Calitti and Roberto Gigliucci, 2:553–68. Rome: Bulzoni.

Bergemann, Lutz, Martin Dönike, Albert Schirrmeister, Georg Toepfer, Marco Walter, and Julia Weitbrecht. 2019. "Transformation: A Concept for the Study of Cultural Change." In *Beyond Reception: Renaissance Humanism and the Transformation of Classical Antiquity*, edited by Patrick Baker, Johannes Helmrath, and Craig Kallendorf, 9–26. Berlin: De Gruyter.

Berger, Andreas. 2002. *Die* Meleagris *des Basinio Basini: Einleitung, kritische Edition, Übersetzung, Kommentar*. Trier: Wissenschaftlicher Verlag.

Bietenholz, Peter G., and Thomas Brian Deutscher, eds. 2003. *Contemporaries of Erasmus: A Biographical Register of the Renaissance and Reformation*. Toronto: University of Toronto Press.

Bloemendal, Jan, ed. 2015. *Bilingual Europe: Latin and Vernacular Cultures – Examples of Bilingualism and Multilingualism c. 1300–1800*. Leiden: Brill.

Bouscharain, Anne. 2006. "Les Traductions françaises des *carmina* de Battista Spagnoli." In *L'Italie et la France dans l'Europe latine du XIVᵉ au XVIIᵉ siècle: Influence, émulation, traduction*, edited by Marc Deramaix and Ginette Vagenheim, 397–415. Rouen: Presses universitaires de Rouen et du Havre.

Burrow, Colin. 2019. *Imitating Authors: Plato to Futurity*. Oxford: Oxford University Press.

Cardini, Roberto. 1973. *La critica del Landino*. Florence: Sansoni.

Chappuis Sandoz, Laure. 2011. *Au-delà de l'élégie d'amour: métamorphoses et renouvellements d'un genre latin dans l'antiquité et à la Renaissance*. Paris: Classiques Garnier.

Charlet, Jean-Louis. 1997. "Eros et érotisme dans la *Cinthia* d'Enea Silvio Piccolomini." In *Éros et Priapus: érotisme et obscénité dans la littérature néo-latine*, edited by Philip Ford and Ingrid de Smet, 1–23. Geneva: Droz.

Charlet, Jean-Louis. 2007. "État présent des recherches sur la poésie latine d'Enea Silvio Piccolomini." In *Pio II umanista europeo. (Atti del XVII convegno internazionale, Chianciano-Pienza, 18–21 Luglio 2005)*, edited by L. Secchi Tarugi, 81–88. Florence: Cesati.

Charlet, Jean-Louis. 2011. "Les Élégies introspectives de Giovannantonio Campano." In *Au-delà de l'élégie d'amour: métamorphoses et renouvellements d'un genre latin dans l'Antiquité et à la Renaissance*, edited by Laure Chappuis Sandoz, 209–28. Paris: Classiques Garnier.

Chines, Loredana, Floriana Calitti, and Roberto Gigliucci, eds. 2006. *Il Petrarchismo: un modello di poesia per l'Europa*. 2 vols. Rome: Bulzoni.

Cinti, Federico. 2006. "Per un atlante del petrarchismo neolatino europeo." In *Il Petrarchismo: un modello di poesia per l'Europa.*, edited by Floriana Calitti and Roberto Gigliucci, 2:499–516. Rome: Bulzoni.

Comiati, Giacomo. 2018. "The Reception of Petrarch and Petrarchists' Poetry in Marcantonio Flaminio's *Carmina.*" In *Neo-Latin and the Vernaculars: Bilingual Interactions in the Early Modern Period*, edited by Florian Schaffenrath and Alexander Winkler, 188–211. Leiden: Brill.

Conte, Gian Biagio. 1989. "Love without Elegy: The *Remedia Amoris* and the Logic of a Genre." Translated by Glenn W. Most. *Poetics Today* 10 (3): 441–69.

Coppini, Donatella. 2000. "Ritratti al femminile nella poesia latina del Quattrocento." In *Immaginare l'autore: il ritratto del letterato nella cultura umanistica. Convegno di studi, Firenze, 26–27 marzo 1998*, edited by Giovanna Lazzi and Paolo Viti, 291–327. Florence: Polistampa.

Coppini, Donatella. 2006. "I canzonieri latini del Quattrocento : Petrarca e l'epigramma nella strutturazione dell'opera elegiaca." In *"Liber", "fragmenta", "libellus". Prima e dopo Petrarca. In ricordo di d'Arco Silvio Avalle*, edited by Francesco Lo Monaco, Luca Carlo Rossi, and Niccolò Scaffai, 209–38. Florence: Tavarnuzze.

Coppini, Donatella. 2009. "Basinio da Parma e l'elegia epistolare." In *Il Rinnovamento umanistico della poesia. L'epigramma e l'elegia*, edited by Donatella Coppini and Roberto Cardini, 281–302. Florence: Polistampa.

Coppini, Donatella. 2020. "'Mentula, cunnus abest': La critica dell'osceno in termini osceni nelle polemiche contro Il Panormita." In *Spheres of Conflict and Rivalries in Renaissance Europe*, edited by David A. Lines, Marc Laureys, and Jill Kraye, 22–44. Bonn: Bonn University Press.

Coppini, Donatella, and Roberto Cardini, eds. 2009. *Il Rinnovamento umanistico della poesia. L'epigramma e l'elegia*. Florence: Polistampa.

Coppini, Donatella, and Michele Feo, eds. 2012. *Petrarca, l'umanesimo e la civiltà europea: atti del convegno internazionale, Firenze, 5–10 dicembre 2004*. Florence: Le Lettere.

Cox, Virginia. 2005. "Sixteenth-Century Women Petrarchists and the Legacy of Laura." *Journal of Medieval and Early Modern Studies* 35 (3): 583–606.

Cox, Virginia. 2008. *Women's Writing in Italy, 1400–1650*. Baltimore: Johns Hopkins University Press.

Cummings, Robert. 2017. "Epigram." In *A Guide to Neo-Latin Literature*, edited by Victoria Moul, 83–97. Cambridge: Cambridge University Press.

Czapla, Beate. 2006. "Sannazaros zweite Ekloge *Galatea* als Neufassung eines *non ignobile carmen* (Vergil Ecl. 9. 37–43)." In *Sannazaro und die Augusteische Dichtung*, edited by Eckart Schäfer, 69–86. Tübingen: Narr.

Dall'Orto, Giovanni. 2002. "Massimi, Pacifico." In *Who's Who in Gay and Lesbian History: From Antiquity to the Mid-Twentieth Century*, edited by Robert Aldrich and Garry Wotherspoon, 356–57. London: Routledge.

Dauvois, Nathalie, Michel Jourde, and Jean-Charles Monferran, eds. 2019. *Chacun son Horace: appropriations et adaptations du modèle horatien en Europe (XVᵉ–XVIIᵉ siècles)*. Paris: Champion.

De Beer, Susanna. 2010. "Ghostwriting in the Renaissance? Giannantonio Campano's Love Elegies for 'Diana', the Mistress of Braccio Baglioni." *Neulateinisches Jahrbuch: Journal of Neo-Latin Language and Literature* 12: 41–65.

De Beer, Susanna. 2013. *The Poetics of Patronage: Poetry as Self-Advancement in Giannantonio Campano*. Turnhout: Brepols.

De Beer, Susanna. 2014. "Elegiac Poetry." In *Brill's Encyclopaedia of the Neo-Latin World*. Leiden: Brill.

De Beer, Susanna, K. A. E. Enenkel, and David Rijser, eds. 2009. *The Neo-Latin Epigram: A Learned and Witty Genre*. Leuven: Leuven University Press.

Debrohun, Jeri Blair. 2003. *Roman Propertius and the Reinvention of Elegy*. Ann Arbor: University of Michigan Press.

Della Torre, Arnaldo. 1902. *Storia dell'Accademia platonica di Firenze*. Florence: G. Carnesecchi.

Deneire, Thomas, ed. 2014. *Dynamics of Neo-Latin and the Vernacular: Language and Poetics, Translation and Transfer*. Leiden: Brill.

De Nichilo, Mauro. 1999. "Le 'Elegie' per Giulia di Francesco Ottavio Cleofilo." In *Poesia umanistica latina in distici elegiaci*, edited by Giuseppe Catanzaro and Francesco Santucci, 251–88. Assisi: Accademia Properziana del Subasio di Assisi.

Descoings, Karine. 2009. "Défense et illustration d'Amour en poésie dans les *Tristes* d'Ovide et dans les *Schediasmata Poetica* du poète néo-latin Paul Schede Melissus." *Rursus. Poétique, réception et réécriture des textes antiques*, no. 4 (February).

Desjardins, Juliette. 1979. "Un document sur la crise morale du Quattrocento : L'*Hecatelegium* de Pacifico Massimi d'Ascoli." *Réforme, Humanisme, Renaissance* 9 (1): 20–36.

Dettmer, Helena. 1997. *Love by the Numbers: Form and Meaning in the Poetry of Catullus*. New York: P. Lang.

Dörrie, Heinrich. 1968. *Der heroische Brief; Bestandsaufnahme, Geschichte, Kritik einer humanistisch-barocken Literaturgattung*. Berlin: De Gruyter.

Eickmeyer, Jost. 2014. "Imitating Ovid to the Greater Glory of God: Jesuit Poets and Christian Heroic Epistles (1514–1663)." *Journal of Jesuit Studies* 1 (3): 419–42.

Eisenbichler, Konrad, ed. 2009. *Renaissance Medievalisms*. Tempe, AZ: Centre for Reformation and Renaissance Studies.

Endres, Clifford. 1981. *Joannes Secundus: The Latin Love Elegy in the Renaissance*. Hamden, CT: Archon Books.

Enenkel, Karl. 2014. "Neo-Latin Erotic and Pornographic Literature (c. 1400–c. 1700)." In *Brill's Encyclopaedia of the Neo-Latin World*, 487–501. Leiden: Brill.

Enenkel, Karl, and Jan Papy, eds. 2006. *Petrarch and His Readers in the Renaissance*. Leiden: Brill.

Fantazzi, Charles. 1996. "The Style of Quattrocento Latin Love Poetry." *International Journal of the Classical Tradition* 3 (2): 127–46.

Fantham, Elaine. 2013. *Roman Literary Culture: From Plautus to Macrobius*. Baltimore: Johns Hopkins University Press.

Ferguson, Gary. 2008. *Queer (Re)Readings in the French Renaissance: Homosexuality, Gender, Culture*. Aldershot: Ashgate.

Ferroni, Giovanni. 2012. *Dulces lusus: lirica pastorale e libri di poesia nel Cinquecento*. Edizioni dell'Orso.

Ford, Philip. 1993. "The Basia of Johannes Secundus and Lyon Poetry." In *Intellectual Life in Renaissance Lyon*, edited by Philip Ford and Gillian Jondorf, 113–33. Cambridge: Cambridge French Colloquia.

Ford, Philip. 1997. "Jean Salmon Macrin's *Epithalamiorum Liber* and the Joys of Conjugal Love." In *Éros et Priapus*, edited by Ingrid De Smet and Philip Ford, 64–84. Geneva: Droz.

Ford, Philip. 2011. "Obscenity and the *lex catulliana*: Uses and Abuses of Catullus 16 in French Renaissance Poetry." In *Obscénités renaissantes*, edited by Hugh Roberts, Lise Wajeman, and Guillaume Peureux, 48–60. Geneva: Droz.

Ford, Philip. 2013. *The Judgment of Palaemon: The Contest Between Neo-Latin and Vernacular Poetry in Renaissance France*. Leiden: Brill.

Ford, Philip and Ingrid De Smet, eds. 1997. *Éros et Priapus: érotisme et obscénité dans la littérature néo-latine*. Geneva: Droz.

Ford, Philip and Andrew Taylor, eds. 2006. *Neo-Latin and the Pastoral*. Vol. 33. Canadian Review of Comparative Literature. Edmonton: Canadian Comparative Literature Association.

Forster, Leonard. 1969. *The Icy Fire: Five Studies in European Petrarchism*. Cambridge: Cambridge University Press.

Forster, Leonard. 1978. "Some Examples of Petrarchism in Latin in Slavonic Lands." *Humanistica Lovaniensia* 27: 1–9.

Fredericksen, Erik. 2014. "Jacopo Sannazaro's 'Piscatory Eclogues' and the Question of Genre." *New Voices in Classical Reception Studies* 9.

Fredericksen, Erik. 2015. "Finding Another Alexis: Pastoral Tradition and the Reception of Vergil's Second Eclogue." *Classical Receptions Journal* 7 (3): 422–41.

Gaisser, Julia Haig. 1993. *Catullus and His Renaissance Readers*. Oxford: Clarendon Press ; Oxford University Press.

Gaisser, Julia Haig. 2012. *Catullus*. New York: Wiley-Blackwell.

Gaisser, Julia Haig. 2015. "Pontano's Catullus." In *What Catullus Wrote: Problems in Textual Criticism, Editing and the Manuscript Tradition*, edited by Dániel Kiss, 53–92. Swansea: Classical Press of Wales.

Gaisser, Julia Haig. 2017. "Lyric." In *A Guide to Neo-Latin Literature*, edited by Victoria Moul, 113–30. Cambridge: Cambridge University Press.

Gaisser, Julia Haig. 2019. "Excuses, Excuses: The Fortunes of Catullus 16 from Martial to Johannes Secundus." *Paideia: Rivista di filologia, ermeneutica e critica letteraria* LXXIV: 1325–60.

Galand, Perrine. 1993. "La Poétique de jeunesse de Pie II: la *Cinthia*." *Latomus* 52 (4): 875–96.

Galand, Perrine. 1995. *Les yeux de l'éloquence: poétiques humanistes de l'évidence*. Paradigme.

Galand, Perrine. 1998. "Jean Salmon Macrin et la liberté de l'éloge." In *Cultura e potere nel Rinascimento: atti del IX convegno internazionale (Chianciano-Pienza 21–24 Luglio 1997)*, edited by Luisa Secchi Tarugi, 515–29. Florence: Franco Cesati.

Galand, Perrine. 2010. "Jean Second émule des poètes néo-latins italiens dans les *Basia*." In *Gli antichi e i moderni: Studi in onore di Roberto Cardini*, edited by Lucia Bertolini, Donatella Coppini, and Roberto Cardini, 651–72. Florence: Polistampa.

Galand, Perrine, and Jean Balsamo, eds. 2000. *Petrarca, l'umanesimo e la civiltà europea*. Paris: Belles lettres / Klincksieck.

Galand, Perrine, and John Nassichuk, eds. 2011. *Aspects du lyrisme conjugal à la Renaissance*. Geneva: Droz.

Gardner, Hunter H. 2013. *Gendering Time in Augustan Love Elegy*. Oxford: Oxford University Press.

Gärtner, Thomas. 2015. "Der strukturelle Aufbau der *Amores* des Konrad Celtis vor dem Hintergrund aniker Vorbilder." In *Würzburger Humanismus*, edited by Thomas Baier and Jochen Schultheiss, 37–45. Tübingen: Narr.

Genton, Hervé. 2007. "Histoire des reproches adressés aux *Poemata* de Bèze par les polémistes luthériens." In *Théodore de Bèze, (1519–1605): actes du colloque de Genève (septembre 2005)*, edited by Irena Dorota Backus, 163–73. Geneva: Droz.

Gibson, Roy K. 2007. *Excess and Restraint: Propertius, Horace and Ovid's* Ars Amatoria. London: Institute of Classical Studies.

Gillespie, Stuart. 2021. "Early Modern Sapphos in France and England." In *The Cambridge Companion to Sappho*, edited by Adrian Kelly and P. J. Finglass, 332–42. Cambridge: Cambridge University Press.

Godman, Peter. 1988. "Johannes Secundus and Renaissance Latin Poetry." *The Review of English Studies* 39 (154): 258–72.

Goldschmidt, Nora. 2019. *Afterlives of the Roman Poets: Biofiction and the Reception of Latin Poetry*. Cambridge: Cambridge University Press.

Grafton, Anthony. 1994. *Defenders of the Text: The Traditions of Scholarship in an Age of Science, 1450–1800*. Cambridge, MA: Harvard University Press.

Grant, Linda. 2019. *Latin Erotic Elegy and the Shaping of Sixteenth-Century English Love Poetry: Lascivious Poets*. Cambridge: Cambridge University Press.

Grant, W. Leonard. 1955. "Early Neo-Latin Pastoral." *Phoenix* 9 (1): 19–26.

Grant, W. Leonard. 1956. "Later Neo-Latin Pastoral: I." *Studies in Philology* 53 (3): 429–51.

Grant, W. Leonard. 1957a. "Later Neo-Latin Pastoral: II." *Studies in Philology* 54 (4): 481–97.

Grant, W. Leonard. 1957b. "New Forms of Neo-Latin Pastoral." *Studies in the Renaissance* 4: 71–100.

Grant, W. Leonard. 1965. *Neo-Latin Literature and the Pastoral.* University of North Carolina Press.

Greene, Ellen. 2010. *The Erotics of Domination: Male Desire and the Mistress in Latin Love Poetry.* Norman: University of Oklahoma Press.

Guillet-Laburthe, Suzanne. 2011. "De la Nymphe à la Sainte. Continuité et discontinuité de la représentation de l'épouse dans les *Œuvres* de Jean Salmon Macrin." In *Aspects du lyrisme conjugal à la Renaissance*, edited by Perrine Galand and John Nassichuk, 89–124. Geneva: Droz.

Guillot, Roland. 2011. *Essais sur Jean Second.* Paris: Classiques Garnier.

Gutzwiller, Kathryn, ed. 2005. *The New Posidippus: A Hellenistic Poetry Book.* Oxford: Oxford University Press.

Hankins, James. 2012. "Petrarch and the Canon of Neo-Latin Literature." In *Petrarca, l'umanesimo e la civiltà europea: atti del convegno internazionale, Firenze, 5–10 dicembre 2004*, edited by Donatella Coppini and Michele Feo, 905–22. Florence: Le Lettere.

Hardie, Philip. 2002. *Ovid's Poetics of Illusion.* Cambridge: Cambridge University Press.

Haynes, Kenneth. 2007. "The Modern Reception of Greek Epigram." In *Brill's Companion to Hellenistic Epigram*, edited by Peter Bing and Jon Steffen Bruss, 565–83. Leiden: Brill.

Heckel, Iris, ed. 2014. *Floris van Schoonhoven: Lalage sive Amores Pastorales – Lalage oder Bukolische Liebesgedichte (1613).* Tübingen: Narr Francke Attempto Verlag.

Heesakkers, Chris L. 1975. "Petrus Scriverius as the Publisher of the *Poemata* of Janus Dousa." *Quaerendo* 5 (2): 105–25.

Hock, Jessie. 2021. *The Erotics of Materialism: Lucretius and Early Modern Poetics.* University of Pennsylvania Press.

Hollewand, Karen. 2021. "Sex and the Classics: The Approaches of Early Modern Humanists to Ancient Sexuality." In *The Worlds of Knowledge and the Classical Tradition in the Early Modern Age*, edited by Dmitri Levitin and Ian Maclean, 63–90. Leiden: Brill.

Houghton, Luke B. T. 2013. "Renaissance Latin Love Elegy." In *The Cambridge Companion to Latin Love Elegy*, edited by Thea S. Thorsen, 290–305. Cambridge Companions to Literature. Cambridge: Cambridge University Press.

Houghton, Luke B. T. 2017. "Elegy." In *A Guide to Neo-Latin Literature*, edited by Victoria Moul, 98–112. Cambridge: Cambridge University Press.

Hubbard, Thomas K. 1983. "The Catullan Libellus." *Philologus* 127 (1–2): 218–37.

Hutton, James. 1935. *The Greek Anthology in Italy to the Year 1800*. Ithaca, NY: Cornell University Press.

Hutton, James. 1946. *The Greek Anthology in France and in the Latin Writers of the Netherlands to the Year 1800*. Ithaca, NY: Cornell University Press.

James, Sharon L. 2003. *Learned Girls and Male Persuasion: Gender and Reading in Roman Love Elegy*. Berkeley: University of California Press.

Jankovits, László. 2014. "Janus Pannonius' Andromeda Poem as an Ethopoeia." *Colloquia Maruliana* 23 (23): 12–12.

Keith, Alison. 2001. "Ovidian Allusion in Lotichius' Callirhoë Elegies." In *Lotichius und die römische Elegie*, edited by Ulrike Auhagen and Eckart Schäfer, 135–51. Tübingen: Narr.

Kennedy, Duncan F. 1993. *The Arts of Love: Five Studies in the Discourse of Roman Love Elegy*. Cambridge: Cambridge University Press.

Kidwell, Carol. 1989. *Marullus: Soldier Poet of the Renaissance*. London: Duckworth.

Kofler, Wolfgang, and Anna Novokhatko, eds. 2016. *Cristoforo Landinos "Xandra" und die Transformationen römischer Liebesdichtung im Florenz des Quattrocento*. Tübingen: Narr.

Koopmans, Jelle. 2021. "Even in Latin … Deterritorializations of the Obscene." In *The Politics of Obscenity in the Age of the Gutenberg Revolution: Obscene Means in Early Modern French and European Print Culture and Literature*, edited by Peter Frei and Nelly Labère. New York: Routledge.

Kraszewski, Charles S. 2006. "Maciej Kazimierz Sarbiewski: The Christian Horace in England." *The Polish Review* 51 (1): 15–40.

Kraye, Jill. 1994. "The Transformation of Platonic Love in the Italian Renaissance." In *Platonism and the English Imagination*, edited by Anna Baldwin and Sarah Hutton, 76–85. Cambridge: Cambridge University Press.

Lamers, Han. 2009. "Marullo's Imitations of Catullus in the Context of His Poetical Criticism." In *The Neo-Latin Epigram. A Learned and Witty Genre*, edited by Susanna de Beer, Karl Enenkel, and David Rijser, 191–213. Leuven: Leuven University Press.

Landi, Ilaria. 2006. "I *Rerum vulgarium fragmenta* tra i modelli dell'elegia senese e fiorentina del Quattrocento." In *Il Petrarchismo: un modello di poesia per l'Europa*, edited by Floriana Calitti and Roberto Gigliucci, 2:517–52. Rome: Bulzoni.

Laureys, Marc, Nathalie Dauvois, and Donatella Coppini, eds. 2020. *Non omnis moriar: Die Horaz-Rezeption in der neulateinischen Literatur vom 15. bis zum 17. Jahrhundert. (Deutschland – France – Italia)*. Georg Olms Verlag.

Lefèvre, Eckard, and Eckart Schäfer, eds. 2009. *Ianus Dousa: neulateinischer Dichter und klassischer Philologe*. Tübingen: Narr.

Leroux, Virginie. 2015. "Le Baiser et le Songe: enjeux intertextuels et génériques de l'imitation de Jean Second dans les *Juvenilia* de Marc-Antoine Muret." In *Die neulateinische Dichtung in Frankreich zur Zeit der Pléiade*, edited by Marie-France Guipponi-Gineste, Wolfgang Kofler, Anna Novokhatko, and Gilles Polizzi, 63–77. Tübingen: Narr.

Leroux, Virginie. 2021. "Le Lyrisme anti-conjugal dans l'élégie néo-latine." *Camenae* 27: 1–18.

Lionetto, Adeline, ed. 2021. *Le Mariage à la Renaissance.* Camenae 27 (December 2021). http://saprat.ephe.sorbonne.fr/revue-en-ligne-camenae-16.htm.

Ludwig, Walther. 1976. "Petrus Lotichius Secundus and the Roman Elegists: Prolegomena to a Study of Neo-Latin Elegy." In *Classical Influences on European Culture AD 1500–1700*, edited by R. R. Bolgar, 171–90. Cambridge: Cambridge University Press.

Ludwig, Walther. 1989a. "Catullus renatus: Anfänge und frühe Entwicklung des catullischen Stils in der neulateinischen Dichtung." In *Litterae Neolatinae: Schriften zur Neulateinischen Literatur*, edited by Walther Ludwig and Ludwig Braun, 162–94. Munich: W. Fink.

Ludwig, Walther. 1989b. "Platons Kuß und seine Folgen." *Illinois Classical Studies* 14 (1/2): 435–47.

Ludwig, Walther. 1990. "The Origin and Development of the Catullan Style in Neo-Latin Poetry." In *Latin Poetry and the Classical Tradition: Essays in Medieval and Renaissance Literature*, edited by Peter Godman and Oswyn Murray, 183–97. Oxford: Clarendon Press.

Ludwig, Walther. 1991. "The Beginnings of Catullan Neo-Latin Poetry." In *Acta Conventus Neo-Latini Torontonensis: Proceedings of the Seventh International Congress of Neo-Latin Studies*, edited by Alexander Dalzell, Charles Fantazzi, and Richard Schoeck, 449–56. Binghampton, NY: MRTS.

Lyne, R. O. A. M. 1979. "Servitium amoris." *The Classical Quarterly* 29 (1): 117–30.

Macaskill, Annick. 2015. "'C'est un amour ou Cupidon nouveau': Spiritual Passion and the Profane Persona in Anne de Marquets's *Les Divines Poesies de Marc Antoine Flaminius* (1568–1569)." *Renaissance and Reformation / Renaissance et Réforme* 38 (3): 61–81.

Maddison, Carol. 1965. *Marcantonio Flaminio, Poet, Humanist and Reformer.* Chapel Hill: University of North Carolina Press.

Mathieu-Castellani, Gisèle, ed. 1980. *La Métamorphose dans la poésie baroque française et anglaise: variations et résurgences: actes du colloque international de Valenciennes, 1979.* Tübingen: Narr.

Mathieu-Castellani, Gisèle, ed.1981. *Mythes de l'Éros Baroque.* Paris: Presses universitaires de France.

McFarlane, I. D. 1959. "Jean Salmon Macrin (1490–1557)." *Bibliothèque d'Humanisme et Renaissance* 21–22: 55–84, 311–49, 73–89.

McLaughlin, Martin L. 1995. *Literary Imitation in the Italian Renaissance: The Theory and Practice of Literary Imitation in Italy from Dante to Bembo.* New York, Oxford: Clarendon Press.

McNair, Bruce. 2018. *Cristoforo Landino: His Works and Thought*. Leiden: Brill.

Mertz, James J., ed. 1989. *Jesuit Latin Poets of the 17th and 18th Centuries: An Anthology of Neo-Latin Poetry*. Wauconda, IL: Bolchazy-Carducci Publishers.

Mesdjian, Béatrice. 1997. "Éros dans l'*Eroticon* de T. V. Strozzi." In *Eros et Priapus: érotisme et obscénité dans la littérature néo-latine*, edited by Ingrid De Smet and Philip Ford, 25–42. Geneva: Droz.

Michelakis, Pantelis. 2009. "Greek Lyric from the Renaissance to the Eighteenth Century." In *The Cambridge Companion to Greek Lyric*, edited by Felix Budelmann, 336–51. Cambridge: Cambridge University Press.

Miller, Paul Allen. 2004. *Subjecting Verses: Latin Love Elegy and the Emergence of the Real*. Princeton: Princeton University Press.

Mindt, Nina. 2017. "The Inner-Poetic History of Latin Love Poetry in Tito Vespasiano Strozzi's *Eroticon*." In *Renaissance Rewritings*, edited by Helmut Pfeiffer, Irene Fantappiè, and Tobias Roth. Berlin: De Gruyter.

Montoya, Alicia C., Sophie van Romburgh, and Wim van Anrooij, eds. 2010. *Early Modern Medievalisms: The Interplay between Scholarly Reflection and Artistic Production*. Leiden: Brill.

Morrison, Mary. 1955. "Catullus in the Neo-Latin Poetry of France Before 1550." *Bibliothèque d'Humanisme et Renaissance* 17 (3): 365–94.

Moul, Victoria. 2013. "English Elegies of the Sixteenth and Seventeenth Century." In *The Cambridge Companion to Latin Love Elegy*, edited by Thea S. Thorsen, 306–19. Cambridge: Cambridge University Press.

Moul, Victoria. 2015. "Lyric Poetry." In *The Oxford Handbook of Neo-Latin*, edited by Sarah Knight and Stefan Tilg, 41–56. Oxford: Oxford University Press.

Mulas, Alessandra. 2009. "Per l'*Hecatelegium primum* di Pacifico Massimi." *Letteratura Italiana Antica : Rivista Annuale Di Testi e Studi*, no. 10: 1000–1022.

Mundt, Lothar. 1991. "Zu den *Amores* (1542) des Simon Lemnius." In *Acta Conventus Neo-Latini Torontonensis: Proceedings of the Seventh International Congress of Neo-Latin Studies: Toronto, 8 August to 13 August, 1988*, edited by Charles Fantazzi, Richard J Schoeck, and Alexander Dalzell, 519–28. Binghamton, NY: Medieval & Renaissance Texts & Studies.

Murgatroyd, P. 1997. "The Similes at Tito Strozzi *Erotica* 1.3.1ff." *Bibliothèque d'Humanisme et Renaissance* 59 (1): 57–62.

Murgatroyd, Paul. 1981. "'Seruitium amoris' and the Roman Elegists." *Latomus* 40 (Fasc. 3): 589–606.

Nassichuk, John. 2008. "La condition tragique de l'homme dans la Silve IV des *Juvenilia* de Théodore de Bèze." *Études françaises* 44 (2): 85–105.

Nassichuk, John. 2015. "Proteus and the Pursuit of Cupid: The Final Poem of Nicolas Brizard's *Metamorphoses Amoris* (1556)." In *Allusions and Reflections: Greek and Roman Mythology in Renaissance Europe*, edited by Elisabeth Wåghäll Nivre, 363–80. Newcastle upon Tyne: Cambridge Scholars Publishing.

Nassichuk, John. 2021. "*Lex conjugii*: Imitation poétique et chant matrimonial chez Giovanni Pontano." *Camenae* 27: 1–20.

Nichols, Fred J. 1998. "Navagero's *Lusus* and the Pastoral Tradition." In *Acta Conventus Neo-Latini Bariensis: Proceedings of the Ninth International Congress of Neo-Latin Studies*, edited by Rhoda Schnur, J. F. Alcina, John Dillon, Walther Ludwig, Colette Nativel, Mauro De Nichilo, and Stephen Ryle, 445–52. Tempe, AZ: Medieval & Renaissance Texts & Studies.

Norbrook, David, S. J. Harrison, and Philip R. Hardie. 2016. *Lucretius and the Early Modern*. Oxford University Press.

O'Brien, John. 1995. *Anacreon Redivivus: A Study of Anacreontic Translation in Mid-Sixteenth-Century France*. Ann Arbor: University of Michigan Press.

Orth, Christian. 2008. "Daniel Heinsius und die griechische Literatur: Das Abschiedsgedicht an Rossa (*Monobiblos* 10)." In *Daniel Heinsius. Klassischer Philologe und Poet*, edited by Eckard Lefèvre and Eckart Schäfer, 127–43. Tübingen: Narr.

Paleit, Edward. 2008. "Sexual and Political Liberty and Neo-Latin Poetics: The *Heroides* of Mark Alexander Boyd." *Renaissance Studies* 22 (3): 351–67.

Palmer, Ada. 2014. *Reading Lucretius in the Renaissance*. Cambridge, MA: Harvard University Press.

Panizza, Letizia. 2011. "Platonic Love on the Rocks: Castiglione Counter-Currents in Renaissance Italy." In *Laus Platonici Philosophi: Marsilio Ficino and His Influence*, edited by Peter J. Forshaw, Valery Rees, and Stephen Clucas, 199–226. Leiden: Brill.

Parker, Holt N. 2012. "Renaissance Latin Elegy." In *A Companion to Roman Love Elegy*, edited by Barbara K. Gold, 476–90. Oxford: Wiley-Blackwell.

Piantanida, Cecilia. 2021. "Early Modern and Modern German, Italian, and Spanish Sapphos." In *The Cambridge Companion to Sappho*, edited by Adrian Kelly and P. J. Finglass, 343–60. Cambridge: Cambridge University Press.

Pieper, C. H. 2018. "Epic Challenges. Basinio Da Parma's Cyris and the Discourse of Genre in Early Humanistic Elegy." In *Tradição e Transformação. A Herança Latina no Renascimento*, edited by E. C. Santorelli, Lima R. da Cunha, R. T. Casila, and T. A. Napoli, 121–47. Sao Paulo: Editora Humanitas.

Pieper, Christoph. 2008. *Elegos redolere Vergiliosque sapere: Cristoforo Landinos "Xandra" zwischen Liebe und Gesellschaft*. Hildesheim: Olms.

Pieper, Christoph. 2009. "Genre Negotiations: Cristoforo Landino's *Xandra* between Elegy and Epigram." In *The Neo-Latin Epigram: A Learned and Witty Genre*, edited by Susanna de Beer, K. A. E. Enenkel, and David Rijser, 165–90. Leuven: Leuven University Press.

Pieper, Christoph. 2010. "Medievalisms In Latin Love Poetry Of The Early Italian Quattrocento." In *Early Modern Medievalisms*, edited by Alicia C. Montoya, Sophie van Romburgh, and Wim van Anrooij, 45–65. Leiden: Brill.

Piepho, Lee, ed. 1989a. *Adulescentia: The Eclogues of Mantuan*. New York: Garland.

Piepho, Lee, ed. 1989b. "Mantuan on Women and Erotic Love: A Newly Discovered Manuscript of the Unprinted Version of His Eclogues." *Renaissance Studies* 3 (1): 13–28.

Piepho, Lee, ed. 2006. "Mantuan Revised: His *Adulescentia* in Early Sixteenth-Century Germany." In *Neo-Latin and the Pastoral*, edited by Philip Ford and Andrew Taylor, 33:60–74. Canadian Review of Comparative Literature. Edmonton: Canadian Comparative Literature Association.

Pittaluga, Stefano. 2011. "La *Cinthia* di Enea Silvio Piccolomini. Note di lettura." *Cahiers d'études italiennes*, no. 13 (October): 37–44.

Prescott, Anne Lake. 1974. "English Writers and Beza's Latin Epigrams: The Uses and Abuses of Poetry." *Studies in the Renaissance* 21: 83–117.

Prescott, Anne Lake. 2016. "From 'Amours' to 'Amores': Francis Thorius Makes Ronsard a Neolatin Lover." In *French Connections in the English Renaissance*, edited by Catherine Gimelli Martin and Hassan Melehy, 161–78. London: Taylor & Francis.

Price, David. 1992. "The Poetics of License in Janus Secundus's *Basia*." *The Sixteenth Century Journal* 23 (2): 289–301.

Price, David. 1996. *Janus Secundus*. Tempe, AZ: Medieval & Renaissance Texts & Studies.

Rees, Valery. 2018. "A Sojourner in Florence: Neoplatonic Themes in the *Hymni Naturales* of Marullus." In *Acta Conventus Neo-Latini Vindobonensis: Proceedings of the Sixteenth International Congress of Neo-Latin Studies (Vienna 2015)*, edited by Astrid Steiner-Weber and Franz Römer, 559–70. Leiden: Brill.

Reeser, Todd W. 2016. *Setting Plato Straight: Translating Ancient Sexuality in the Renaissance*. Chicago: University of Chicago Press.

Robert, Jörg. 2003. *Konrad Celtis und das Projekt der deutschen Dichtung: Studien zur humanistischen Konstitution von Poetik, Philosophie, Nation und Ich*. Tübingen: Niemeyer.

Rosenmeyer, Patricia. 1992. *The Poetics of Imitation: Anacreon and the Anacreontic Tradition*. Cambridge: Cambridge University Press.

Rosenmeyer, Patricia. 2002. "The Greek Anacrontics and Sixteenth-Century French Lyric Poetry." In *The Classical Heritage in France*, edited by Gerald Sandy, 393–424. Leiden: Brill.

Sacré, Dirk. 2021. "Adriaan Reland, *Galatea*: An Introduction." In *The Orient in Utrecht: Adriaan Reland (1676–1718), Arabist, Cartographer, Antiquarian and Scholar of Comparative Religion*, edited by Bart Jaski, Christian Lange, Anna Pytlowany, and Henk J. van Rinsum, 243–77. Leiden: Brill.

Schäfer, Eckart. 2001. "Lotichius' Liebesdichtung – ein Experiment mit dem Leben." In *Lotichius und die römische Elegie*, edited by Ulrike Auhagen and Eckart Schäfer, 241–98. Tübingen: Narr.

Schäfer, Eckart. 2004. *Johannes Secundus und die römische Liebeslyrik*. Tübingen: Narr.

Schaffenrath, Florian. 2017. "Some Considerations on the Poetological Aspects of Basinio Da Parma's *Hesperis*." *Humanistica Lovaniensia* 66: 1–22.

Schoolfield, George Clarence. 1980. *Janus Secundus*. Boston: Twayne.

Schumann, Marie-Françoise. 2009. *Salmon Macrin und sein Werk unter besonderer Berücksichtigung der "Carmina ad Gelonidem" von 1528 und 1530*. Münster: Lit.

Segel, Harold B. 1989. *Renaissance Culture in Poland: The Rise of Humanism, 1470–1543*. Cornell University Press.

Skoie, Mathilde. 2002. *Reading Sulpicia: Commentaries, 1475–1990*. Oxford: Oxford University Press.

Skoie, Mathilde. 2012. "*Corpus Tibullianum*, Book 3." In *A Companion to Roman Love Elegy*, edited by Barbara K. Gold, 86–100. Wiley-Blackwell.

Soranzo, Matteo. 2016. *Poetry and Identity in Quattrocento Naples*. London, New York: Routledge.

Sterritt, D. E. L. 2005. "A Latin Legacy in Louise Labé: Imitation of Tibullus 1.2.89–94." *French Forum* 30 (2): 15–30.

Stevenson, Jane. 2005. *Women Latin Poets: Language, Gender, and Authority, from Antiquity to the Eighteenth Century*. Oxford: Oxford University Press.

Tilg, Stefan. 2014. "Neo-Latin Anacreontic Poetry: Its Shape(s) and Its Significance." In *Imitate Anacreon! Mimesis, Poiesis and the Poetic Inspiration in the Carmina Anacreontea*, 163–98. Berlin: De Gruyter.

Tufte, Virginia. 1970. *The Poetry of Marriage; the Epithalamium in Europe and its Development in England*. Los Angeles: Tinnon-Brown.

Urban-Godziek, Grażyna. 2005. *Elegia renesansowa: przemiany gatunku w Polsce i w Europie*. Krakow: Universitas.

Urban-Godziek, Grażyna. 2015. "Two Polish Renaissance Elegiac Cycles (by Klemens Janicki and Jan Kochanowski) in the Light of the Contemporary European Practice." In *Renaissance and Humanism from the Central-East European Point of View*, edited by Grażyna Urban-Godziek, 261–76. Krakow: Jagiellonian University Press.

van Dam, Harm-Jan. 2008. "Daniel Heinsius' Erstlingswerk: Prolegomena zu einer Edition der *Monobiblos*." In *Daniel Heinsius. Klassischer Philologe und Poet*, edited by Eckard Lefèvre and Eckart Schäfer, 127–43. Tübingen: Narr.

van Dam, Harm-Jan. 2009. "Taking Occasion By The Forelock: Dutch Poets And Appropriation Of Occasional Poems." In *Latinitas Perennis. Volume II: Appropriation and Latin Literature*, edited by Jan Papy, Wim Verbaal, and Yanick Maes, 95–122. Leiden: Brill.

Van Sickle, John. 1980. "The Book-Roll and Some Poetic Conventions of the Poetic Book." *Arethusa* 13: 5–42.

Wasdin, Katherine. 2018. *Eros at Dusk: Ancient Wedding and Love Poetry*. Oxford: Oxford University Press.

Weiss, James Michael. 1984. "The Rhetoric of Friendship: Joannes Hagius's « Life of Petrus Lotichius Secundus »." *Colloquia Germanica* 17 (3/4): 220–34.

White, Paul. 2009. *Renaissance Postscripts: Responding to Ovid's* Heroides *in Sixteenth-Century France*. Columbus: Ohio State University Press.

White, Paul. 2012. "Representation and Illusion in the 'Elegies' of Théodore de Bèze." *French Studies* 66: 1–11.

White, Paul. 2017. "Ronsard's *Continuation des Amours* (1555) in Dialogue with Muret's *Elegiae* (1552)." *Bibliothèque d'Humanisme et Renaissance* 79.1.

White, Paul. 2019. *Gallus Reborn: A Study of the Diffusion and Reception of Works Ascribed to Gaius Cornelius Gallus*. London, New York: Routledge.

Whittington, Leah. 2016. *Renaissance Suppliants: Poetry, Antiquity, Reconciliation*. Oxford: Oxford University Press.

Winkler, Alexander, and Florian Schaffenrath, eds. 2019. *Neo-Latin and the Vernaculars: Bilingual Interactions in the Early Modern Period*. Leiden: Brill.

Wiseman, T. P. 1969. *Catullan Questions*. Leicester: Leicester U.P.

Wong, Alex. 2017. *The Poetry of Kissing in Early Modern Europe: From the Catullan Revival to Secundus, Shakespeare and the English Cavaliers*. Cambridge: D.S. Brewer.

Wong, Alex. 2021. "Catullus in the Renaissance." In *The Cambridge Companion to Catullus*, edited by Ian Du Quesnay and Tony Woodman, 318–42. Cambridge: Cambridge University Press.

Wyke, Maria. 1987. "Written Women: Propertius' *scripta puella*." *The Journal of Roman Studies* 77: 47–61.

Wyke, Maria. 1989. "Mistress and Metaphor in Augustan Elegy." *Helios* 16 (1): 25–47.

Wyke, Maria. 2007. *The Roman Mistress: Ancient and Modern Representations*. Oxford: Oxford University Press.

Zon, Stephen. 1983. *Petrus Lotichius Secundus, Neo-Latin Poet*. Bern: Lang.

Index Nominum

Printed in the United States
by Baker & Taylor Publisher Services